Talk to Me!

Anita Conlan

'I highly recommend this excellent book to every parent, teacher and child. It is both accessible and practical. Anita tackles complex themes with honesty and humanity. The book is littered with interesting anecdotes, illuminating insights and essential advice. She understands contemporary society and human psychology. It demonstrates the compassion and wisdom of many years working in this area with implications for parents and policy-makers alike.'
Feargal Brougham, INTO President

Talk to Me!

Conversations with Teens that Most Parents Would Love to Have

Anita Conlan

ORPEN PRESS

Published by
Orpen Press
Upper Floor, Unit K9
Greenogue Business Park
Rathcoole
Co. Dublin
Ireland

email: info@orpenpress.com
www.orpenpress.com

Paperback ISBN 978-1-78605-078-6
ePub ISBN 978-1-78605-079-3

Printed in Dublin by SPRINTprint Ltd

To all of the students I have worked with over the years – I would like to thank you for your honesty and trust, without which this book could not have been written.

Contents

Foreword xi
Introduction 1

PART I: Pre-Teens: A Fly-On-The-Wall View 3
1. Getting Back in Touch 5
2. Active Listening 10
3. Pressures 15
    School Work 16
    Fitting In 19
    Being Good at Sports or Other Activities 20
    Popularity 21
4. Frequently Identified Worries 24
    Body Developments 24
    Secondary School 25
    Boyfriend/Girlfriend Issues 26
    Dying 26
    Parents Dying 27
    Parents Separating 27
    Violence 28
    Rape/Assault 28
    Being Homeless 29
    Drugs and Drink 29
5. 'The Talk' 31

6. Technology   36
7. Sexual Curiosity   42
8. Intellectual Development..............................   47
    You're Not the Boss of Me!   47
    I'm Not Everybody Else's Parent!...................   48
    Respect Their Opinions...............................   53
9. Emotional Development   56
    Arguments....   58
    Expressing Feelings....................................   59
    Bitchiness   62
    Romantic Interest.....................................   62
    Physical Contact.......................................   65
    Consent...   67
    LGBTQ+ Children   69
    Impact of Parental Arguments and/or Separation ..   73
10. Spiritual Development.................................   77
11. Physical Development.................................   81
    Girls' Development   82
    Boys' Development   91

PART II: Older Teenagers:
A Fly-On-The-Wall View...................................   **97**
12. Topics of Interest   99
13. Expectations of Relationships.........................   101
14. Abusive Relationships.................................   110
15. LGBTQ+ Teens   117
    Sexuality   118
    Transgender Issues   122
16. Sex..   124
    Fear of Failure or 'Not Being Good at It',
      and the Impact of Pornography.....................   126
    Penis Size   128
    Safe Sex...   130
    Consent...   132
    Unplanned Pregnancy................................   136
17. Intimacy   138
18. Mental Health Issues   145
19. The Effect of Drugs and Drink on Relationships ..   151

20. Unplanned Pregnancy 155
21. Toxic Friendships... 158
    Boyfriend/Girlfriend Issues 158
    Jealousy 160
    Disloyalty 161
    Demanding Behaviour... 162
    Competitiveness 162
22. Dealing with Conflict in Relationships 164
    Conflict Styles.. 164
    Dealing with Break-ups or Heartbreak 169
    Family Relationships.. 171
23. Final Thoughts... 175
Useful Contacts 177

Foreword

Fergus Finlay

A few years ago I was doing one of my favourite jobs in Barnardos. I was standing in for Santa Claus. It's a job I love doing so much that I actually have my own top-of-the-range suit with a real leather belt and a wonderful beard. Though I shouldn't say so, I really look the part. I've never met the real Santa, of course, but I'm pretty sure he'd approve of my efforts.

Anyway, we had a wonderful morning in one of the Barnardos projects, with games and presents and the inevitable selection boxes. As it was time for Santa to leave, the kids all gathered around in a semi-circle and sang 'Twinkle, Twinkle Little Star'. Except for one little boy, about four, who stood staring at the floor. I was worried that maybe Santa had done something to upset him, so I asked one of my colleagues if he was ok. 'He's fine', she said, 'but he doesn't know the words.'

In all my life I'd never met a four-year-old who couldn't sing that song, so after the visit I went back to find out a bit more. There were circumstances in this little boy's life that meant he had never been sung to sleep, never had a bedtime story, never had a cuddle before bed. And the team in Barnardos, who are as wise as anyone I've ever met, knew that this was a huge hole in this little boy's life. The absence of that moment in his day was almost a predictor for them of the things that would go wrong for him as he grew older. It became their mission – and it involved intensive work with him and with his mum and dad, who were struggling badly with their own issues – to fill that gap.

That experience – and a whole lot more – taught me something. It was something I should have known better than I did as a parent myself, but it was something I learned watching skilled people at work. That missing moment in a child's life is like a kind of symbol of a bigger point. The key to social and emotional development for a child is often a confident, trusting and open relationship with a grown-up. It really matters when children are very young, and it matters just as much as they grow. In the difficult years, when they're struggling with all sorts of stuff, the knowledge that there is someone there – maybe not someone with all the answers, but someone they can really talk to – matters an awful lot.

Now, Anita Conlan is years younger than me. But I found myself wishing, as I was reading this book, that she had been the grown-up in my life. Because that's what this book is. It's a real adult, helping the rest of us to navigate all the difficult and tricky conversations we have to have with our kids. It's often said that parenting is the most difficult job we ever get asked to do, and the one with the least training. Often, the biggest challenge of all is keeping lines of communication open.

Well, parents everywhere can relax, because help is at hand. Anita is a skilled and experienced educator. She has recently retired after nearly a quarter of a century of running courses in relationships and sexuality education at primary and secondary level, and has distilled everything she knows – including everything she has learned from the mistakes she has made along the way – into this book.

She's had all the conversations. She's covered all the issues that trouble kids along the way. She will say, again and again in the book, that she doesn't know all the answers, but she has learned the value of honesty and directness. And there's no issue that hasn't been covered.

She imparts all that brilliantly. As you read, you learn to trust Anita's judgement, because her open and commonsense approach shines out. You even find yourself thinking, now and again, 'why did that never occur to me?'

I don't know whether I was supposed to say how erudite and learned and technically brilliant this book is. But I'm not going to say that. I think it's especially invaluable because every parent will find it easy to read. You'll recognise the dilemmas you've had to face yourself. Some of the experiences Anita has had will really resonate with you. You'll be really grateful for the tips and tricks Anita offers.

At the heart of the book, and in the title, is a simple but profound thought. No matter what we're going through, we've got to find ways of talking to each other. Our kids have to know we're there for them no matter what, that we trust them and they can trust us. It's never easy, but with Anita at your side, the building of that open and trusting relationship becomes really worthwhile.

Introduction

I was inspired to write this book because of my work in the area of Relationships and Sexuality Education. For approximately 24 years I worked as a facilitator, trainer and programme coordinator in this area. I worked in both the primary and post-primary sector from fifth class to Leaving Cert, and over the years I have worked in hundreds of schools and have had the pleasure of working with tens of thousands of students. It was never a conscious intention to work in the area of Relationship and Sexuality Education, but after training as a facilitator to work with couples preparing them for marriage the opportunity arose for me to retrain to deliver RSE programmes in schools. From my first day in the classroom I was really aware of the value of the work and the more students I spoke to - and more importantly the more students who spoke to me - the more fascinated by the work I became.

A large part of my work involved information evenings for parents and I was frequently asked by them to recommend a book that would be of help when speaking to their children about what quite a few of them thought was a difficult subject and on more than one occasion I was asked why I hadn't written a book myself. So having retired from my role as coordinator of a team delivering RSE I decided the time was right to do just that.

This is not intended to be an instruction manual; as a parent myself I would find that extremely presumptuous. I wanted to offer parents the opportunity of a fly-on-the-wall view of their children's attitudes, worries, hopes and expectations that for all of the obvious reasons are not always discussed as candidly by them at home.

The book is in two sections. Part I covers the years between ten and thirteen, or pre-adolescence, and Part II covers the older teenage years, from thirteen to eighteen.

Although the book is written with parents in mind it could also prove useful to children and teenagers. They would probably rather read a knitting pattern than read the whole book but there may be passages that will prove interesting depending on what is happening in their life at the time.

PART I

Pre-Teens:
A Fly-On-The-Wall
View

Getting Back in Touch

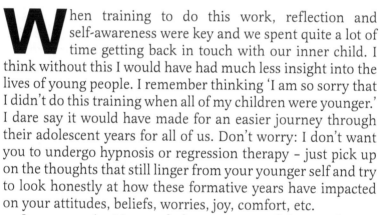

1

When training to do this work, reflection and self-awareness were key and we spent quite a lot of time getting back in touch with our inner child. I think without this I would have had much less insight into the lives of young people. I remember thinking 'I am so sorry that I didn't do this training when all of my children were younger.' I dare say it would have made for an easier journey through their adolescent years for all of us. Don't worry: I don't want you to undergo hypnosis or regression therapy – just pick up on the thoughts that still linger from your younger self and try to look honestly at how these formative years have impacted on your attitudes, beliefs, worries, joy, comfort, etc.

I grew up in Liverpool the youngest of four girls and schooling for me was very definitely of the rote-learning, don't-ask-questions kind usually delivered by very austere, unapproachable teachers. There was no reference to RSE whatsoever until I was about fourteen years old and the nun who taught Domestic Science told us about the importance of hygiene, particularly personal hygiene. The word 'sex' was never mentioned and there was not even a reference to the genitals for that matter. We were left to fill in the blanks by whichever means available, which were very few. There was no Google then! We of course had biology textbooks that described conception and the reproductive organs very briefly and quite unsatisfactorily for a fourteen-year-old girl. You may say 'what about parents' responsibility?' I think my mother would rather have stuck hot needles in her eyes than talk to any of her daughters about anything to do with sex. I had never heard her referring to periods and if there was conversation between adults regarding pregnancy or any kind of procedure involving anything below the waist they were done with gestures, spelling key words and the use of euphemisms. This was the norm until I was about eighteen.

One particularly poignant memory for me was Christmas 1964; I was thirteen years old. For Christmas that year I got a black-and-white op art miniskirt, a Beatles LP, perfume and some money. I had my hair cut in a Mary Quant style. For those of you reading this book who are much younger than me, Mary Quant was a fashion designer in the 60s who was as well known for her iconic hairstyle as her clothes. I had a life-size poster of the Beatles on my bedroom wall, which I kissed every night going to bed, except Ringo! On Christmas night I remember lying in bed feeling very happy with myself, looking at my new clothes hanging on my wardrobe door, when out of the blue came the dawning that Christmas and life in general would never be the same again. I became acutely aware that I was heading towards adulthood. A part of me was delighted with this but there was another part of me that was definitely not. I was interested in all of the usual things for a girl of my age - clothes, friends, the Beatles and boys - but the other part of me still wanted to be a little girl sitting by the fire reading *Little Women* or the *School Friend* annual. I was convinced that I was weird and got really upset; I didn't think for one minute that my friends could possibly have similar feelings. The next morning I decided to tell my mother that I was 'depressed'. Not a good idea, to say the least. This was, after all, Christmas, so I got the talk that always accompanied any kind of dissent at Christmas or family holidays. 'Think of all the poor children; you're just spoiled; look at everything you've got, etc., etc.' I learned one very valuable lesson from that talk and that was never to say I was depressed to my mother again! Of course

I wasn't depressed. I was confused and a bit anxious but not depressed. Naturally the further I got into my teens the desire to run back to childhood grew less and less. Unsurprisingly, a number of children get comfort when I recount this story because they have experienced very similar feelings themselves and it gives them permission to admit to maybe feeling a bit confused and miserable without thinking that there is something weird going on with them. You may or may not have similar memories yourself, and if you do it is a good way to open up a conversation on this topic. In fact, even if you don't you could always pretend you do; we don't always have to be completely honest when we are attempting to illustrate a point.

It is also very common for young people of this age to be overly critical of themselves and others, and I can certainly remember being more than a little dissatisfied with just about every aspect of my being, including the way I looked, the way I walked, my popularity, the way I spoke, my coolness or lack of it, and my knowledge of all things sexual. I could go on but I think you probably get the picture. So you can see the last thing our children want from us is overreaction or us becoming overly anxious with them. They need reassurance and encouragement; not always easy with a stroppy adolescent but if you can manage to get this right at this time it will be the foundation stone for your children as they grow into adults. It often helps to talk about yourself rather than them.

Most of us learn to be parents from observing our own parents. Some people will do their best to replicate what they have seen and others will do their utmost to avoid any similarities. Either way, they have been equally influenced.

So now it is your turn to take a step back into your own adolescence. The following questions may help you to reconnect:

- What did you look like?
- What were your interests?
- If you liked music what was your music of choice?
- Were you popular?

- Did you get on with your parents?
- What was your attitude to matters of the heart? Were you comfortable with the whole romance thing or was there confusion or even worry?
- How was your sexual development handled by your parents?

Then I want you to RELAX! Adolescence is not a terminal condition. This is just another very exciting part of your child's development. It is not a problem to be handled; your children are becoming young adults, not aliens. They are usually both excited and a bit scared about this themselves and the thing they need from us most is reassurance and love.

As you have probably noticed, many children hate to have the spotlight turned on them and find it much easier to have a conversation about somebody else than themselves, so you can talk about yourself, a sibling, a friend, etc. It really doesn't matter as long as you are having the conversation. These examples don't always have to have a fairy-tale ending either where everything ends happily ever after. Nice if they do but not compulsory. You can talk about an incident that maybe did not turn out well for you or an insecurity that you may still have and ask them what they think or what would they suggest if a friend asked their advice. Don't be afraid to let your child know that not everything turns out the way we want it to; that's life and sometimes we can learn more from something not being done perfectly than when it all turns out swimmingly. It is not easy being a parent but neither is it always easy being a child. I remember my son when he was about twelve or thirteen saying 'I wish I was seven.' When I asked him why he said 'things are much simpler when you're seven.' When he said this I had a vague recollection of having similar feelings when I was a child. I would have loved at that moment to take away all of the complications of his life, such as secondary school and puberty, and take him to live in the Outer Hebrides, but I couldn't. The only thing I could do was to explain that whilst it is true that the older we get the more complicated life becomes, hopefully the new possibilities and experiences that accompany this make up for it. He also told me in the same conversation that I was not to tell him that he was not a child. He said he very definitely was a child and intended to stay a child for a very long time. Within approximately one year he would have been extremely offended and probably quite annoyed if I had obeyed his instruction.

So it is fair to say that children are not all little rays of sunshine, especially when they approach this age and more than a few of them can become argumentative, uncommunicative, occasionally sullen and downright rude at times, but my guess is that you have already found this out for yourselves. It is around about the same time that they may even stop liking their parents and they would be more than a little shocked if they discovered that their parents don't always like them either! However, one very valuable piece of advice I was given by an old family friend was 'show them you love them when you least feel like it.' This has a remarkable effect and it can change a volatile situation into a conversation instead of a slanging match. You can do this by a hug, making them a hot drink or just telling them that it doesn't matter how objectionable they try to be you will still love them. That doesn't mean you will necessarily like their behaviour but you love them in spite of it.

Active Listening

2

O
ne commonly held belief, which is not always strictly accurate, is that things are much different now than in previous generations. Well, would that it were true. Without a doubt there is far more readily available information and the fairly recent introduction of Social, Personal and Health Education (SPHE) onto the curriculum in our schools has helped to open conversation, identify some worries and answer some practical questions for students. What it seems it has not done to any great extent is make the conversation between parent and child any easier and it is not uncommon for parents to meet with downright resistance from their children to engage in any conversation that involves talking about body developments, sex, pregnancy, sexuality and any other related topic for that matter. This is probably mainly out of a feeling of awkwardness on the part of both the child and the parent, but is also due to the growing need for privacy in children of this age and this is a boundary line that lots of them do not want their parents to cross.

Yet we are constantly telling parents that they should be able to talk to their children openly about anything. Well of course this is the ideal but I don't think it is helpful to make parents feel inadequate if they have difficulty talking about physical development or any other aspect of hormonal development for that matter, or to think there is something lacking in their parenting skills if their children flatly refuse to engage with them on what is after all a very sensitive subject. Some children are naturally very open and will happily talk about anything but some are far more private by nature and it is unfair to subject these children to a conversation that they find toe-curlingly embarrassing! If you force them to listen you may do more harm than good so forget the nonsense about what you should or should not be doing and let them be the guide. You can tell them that you are aware that that they might feel a bit awkward talking about certain things with you but if they do want to ask you anything or talk about any aspect of development you will do your best to listen and be as helpful as you possibly can. It is okay to tell them that you may be a little embarrassed too or that you may not always have answers because this would normalise their feelings and it allows you to get the answer to a query together if you don't know it off the top of your head.

Some parents prefer to give their child a book that covers developments associated with puberty. I personally would not recommend this as I think the book can sometimes act as a barrier: 'Go away and read this and then we don't have to talk about it again.' Unless, of course, when the book is handed over you explain that you have also read the book and refer them to particular points that you think might be useful or interesting and ask them to come talk to you if they need any clarification. This gives a very clear message that there is nothing shameful or dirty about the subject but you are giving them the space to explore the information on their own and you will be there as back-up if needed.

If anybody asked me was I a good listener when my children were small I would have more than likely said yes, or at least I am most of the time. It was only when I was actually trained in active listening that I realised how mediocre a listener I really was, and if I am honest can still be at times. Parents often have their own agenda when it comes to listening – for instance your child recounts something that happened in school and you may want to use their story to fire off a warning shot should they think of behaving in a similar way. However your child may have some worry or concern that they wanted to talk about but they now just bury it because the atmosphere has changed. So not only do they not get their needs addressed, they may think twice before telling you a similar story. I have definitely been guilty of that one! Or your child says that they don't want to do a particular activity, or they say they are no good at something, to which we may respond 'well you have to do it', or 'don't be silly, just try harder and you'll get good at it.' This can be because we have listened to them or their siblings complaining throughout the day about one thing or another and we have run out of patience or we don't want to let them off the hook too easily for their own good, or it could even be that it is inconvenient for us to change their arrangements. I occasionally talk to children who feel pressured by their parents into participating in various activities. They may even have multiple extracurricular activities on certain days. They may enjoy some of them and blatantly not enjoy others, and when asked why they do so many they frequently say their brothers or sisters have done the same activities or their parents think it would be good for them. These are generally well-meaning parents who want their children to get the most out of life and are happy to invest in helping them to achieve this, but if your child is telling you that they need some time off just listen. Don't immediately think about what that will do to your schedule or even what about their friends who do extra classes in whatever and become more proficient than them. Some things should just be done for fun - and that includes doing nothing at all.

The opposite of this is the child who is always left to their own devices. Their story is completely different and they would often welcome some parental interference or to have some activity arranged for them. The worry with children in this position is that the more unsupervised time they have the more likely they may be to get involved in various risky or dangerous activities. Of course it is not always within the financial reach of all parents to arrange lesson or club fees but where that is the case just taking time out to listen or to go to the park or for a walk can make a world of difference. Some of the happiest memories of my childhood were of building tents on some waste ground next to my house and myself and my friends having a tea party in them, or collecting 'bannymug' (old broken pieces of crockery that we used to dig up out of the ground). If I told my mother I was bored she would invariably say 'go and do something or I'll give you something to do' - and believe me she was not talking about a nice little art project, it would be dishes or dusting. I do think that this made me more inventive but I also know if I had something on my mind I was more likely to discuss it with my eldest sister because she was less dismissive of me.

Why not ask your children if they think you are a good listener? If they say you are ask them how do they know and if they say you are not ask them what you could do to improve your listening skills. Don't get defensive if they say you aren't a good listener; it could be your chance to show them that you are aware that you aren't perfect but are prepared to try to improve.

Do not get hung up on this or it will become false. As I have already said, I have been trained in active listening and I sometimes find myself doing the very opposite of what I know I should be doing. That is because I am not perfect - not a perfect parent or a perfect human being - and that is okay. I just have to be a good enough parent and the best version of me I can be. You may find the following pointers on active listening helpful:

- Pick the right time, not when you are under pressure to do something or be somewhere.
- Try to keep it casual. It is not a counselling session or an interrogation. So maybe if you are driving somewhere or out walking together might be a good time.
- Eye contact is not always helpful as this can make some children a little uncomfortable.
- Feedback what you think you have heard, e.g., 'So am I right in thinking ...?'

- Their answer to the last question may be 'no'. If this is the case ask them to explain which part of the conversation it is that you have misunderstood.
- Thank them for being honest and sharing their opinions and worries with you.

Pressures

3

An important aspect of my work with pre-teens was to encourage them to talk openly about pressures, either real or perceived, associated with this period of their lives. When doing this they routinely identified the following:

- *School work*: this can be pressure from parents, teachers and sometimes themselves.
- *Fitting in*: many children, by the time they reach the start of adolescence, feel 'different' and the need to be accepted becomes more prominent.
- *To be good at sports*: this is not just the normal desire to participate well but a dread of failure. When some children are asked to name something they don't like the children with this fear of failure often say 'I hate losing!'
- *To be popular*: this is not the same as fitting in. It is more a symptom of a child feeling they have to excel at something as simple as getting along with their peers.

These are four of the most common pressures that children are under, so let's have a closer look at what is behind them and maybe explore some possible ways of helping children (and parents) cope with them.

School Work

There is a very fine line between encouragement and pressure. I think you will agree that most parents want their children to reach their potential. Well, the first thing I will say to you is be realistic about their potential. Some children are naturally very academic and studious, some children are very academic but not studious, some children are studious but not very academic, and some children are neither academic nor studious.

Obviously if you are the parent of the child who is both academic and studious you will be delighted, and understandably so. However, the danger with this child is that they can put themselves under quite a lot of pressure and nothing short of perfection will be acceptable to them. It is quite rare that they do not achieve this perfection but this in itself is not necessarily good for someone as far as their emotional development is concerned. I have had experience both professionally and personally of children who just cannot cope with what they see as imperfection in themselves. As parents you obviously don't want to encourage them to underachieve; it would probably be pointless anyway as these children get a great deal of satisfaction from their achievements and why not? What parents can do though is encourage them to do stuff just for the fun of it and if it starts to get competitive you can draw their attention to their competitive nature by using humour, maybe substituting their name with that of their sporting idol and jokingly telling them to lighten up. You know your child and will know what approach would work best with them. If it is school work that they are competitive about maybe tell them about a subject you weren't great at and how in the broader scheme of things it has not been important. After all, as an adult how often are you going to be asked how you did in your school exams? How you do it isn't important; what is important is that they get the message that activities are not necessarily about winning or achieving the highest scores. And remember to resist the urge to brag to friends or family about their achievements (tempting though this may be), especially when they are in earshot.

The child who is academic but not studious can be a challenge to parents, especially if they feel they are not reaching their full potential. This is where the line between nagging and encouragement gets blurred. I should know because I have definitely been guilty of crossing that line in the past. If a child achieves a B in an exam without any study it is very tempting for the parent to say 'you could have gotten an A if you had opened a book', instead of celebrating the B, which is a good mark. I am not suggesting that you encourage them to settle, but nagging just doesn't work; neither does threatening or coercion. The only thing that does work is to encourage them to try their best at whatever they do. Explain that they will not excel at everything and that is ok as long as they don't disappoint themselves through lack of effort. A C from a child who has really worked is more of an accomplishment than an A from a child who did not put any effort in. As the child goes through secondary school, and hopefully to third-level education, the possibility of them achieving good marks without effort becomes slimmer so it is important that they develop a healthy attitude to study and understanding and achieving *their* goals and not their parents' goals.

The child who is not particularly academic but is hardworking often grows into the adult who reaches their full potential. They are quite a rare breed though! Some of these children can sometimes become discouraged when no matter how much work they have put into a particular subject or project they don't get the desired result. It is important when this happens that parents applaud their effort and encourage them not to give up. If they have a particular goal in mind, get them to explore other ways of reaching this goal. There is always more than one way to skin a cat. This can actually be of more benefit to them than achieving the desired result first time around as it teaches them to think outside the box. How often as adults do you hear this strategy encouraged? As with the child who is both academic and studious, these children also may need to be encouraged to lighten up on themselves too. Offer them every encouragement and help if needed but try to ensure that they leave time for socialising, sport or even just watching television for a while. Downtime rejuvenates the brain and they should be encouraged to just have fun.

The child who is neither academic nor studious can often be a worry to parents. I have met children who have come from families that are quite high-achieving yet they do not achieve in an academic way at all. Some of them can feel quite pressured by parents who keep organising extra classes, setting extra homework for them, and discouraging any 'time-wasting' activities such as sport or playing with friends. These children can also have a fear of failure because so much importance is placed on them succeeding. For some the response is not to try at all because in their mind if they don't try they can't fail. It is really important that words such as 'fail' and 'win' are not used with these children. A useful approach to use for these children is to explain that that we all achieve in some ways but just to different levels, at different things and at different times in our lives. For instance, some children can be gifted musically or artistically, or possibly excel at sport, whereas for others their gift may be empathy or having the courage to do the right thing. They may have a gift for humour and this gift will lighten the lives of those around them. Some people who did not reach their full potential as children go on to be very successful adults and vice versa. Again we need to listen to our children so that we really hear what they are interested in and encourage them in this. Too much importance is put on the academic achievement of children to the exclusion of things like art, sport, creative thinking, cooking, and practical abilities such as making something out of nothing, not to mention things like empathy, a sense of social justice, a sense of humour and the ability to communicate with people. If we can concentrate on these qualities instead of attempting solely to rectify their lack of academic ability there is an increased possibility of them growing into well-balanced adults.

FITTING IN

We all want to feel we belong, and never more so than during adolescence. We often look for reassurance from friends and family at this time, maybe because we are becoming aware that we are transitioning from a child into a young adult. We become less familiar to ourselves, not only in the way we look but also in the way we think and feel. I can remember so many conversations with other girls when I was this age about things that were happening to my body that I was not totally sure about and feeling so relieved when they were experiencing similar things. Even though I had three older sisters and a mother I could talk to, I felt more comfortable talking to friends and it was their reassurance I was looking for. As well as worries around body developments, there were also more superficial conversations but nonetheless important, or so I thought at the time, such as comparing hairstyles, clothes and music tastes. I remember very clearly trying to get my hair into the same flicked-out style that the prettiest girl in our group had. I never quite managed it because my hair was a totally different texture but it didn't stop me trying or hoping for validation and, more importantly, dreading not getting it when I was bought something new to wear.

At this time in our lives we very definitely wear a uniform. For me that 'uniform' was attempting to replicate the 'mod' look: monochrome clothes, shift dresses and the signature Mary Quant hairstyle. Now it might be a certain type of running shoe or tracksuit, or a particular designer label, but you can be sure that there is something that is *de rigueur* to the average 11–14-year-old. This can put pressure on parents as some of this can be quite costly. I think if at all possible we should try to encourage our children to be individuals and accept others not by what they wear but by how they are. Having said that, if their request for a certain item of clothing or a particular pair of shoes is within our budget and we are happy to go along with it there is nothing wrong with that. I really do believe though that they should be taught to be discerning and show empathy towards the child who may not be able to afford high fashion.

We should have a conversation with our children about where this high fashion is made and explain to them that a pair of trainers that costs €150 is probably made in the same factory as a pair of trainers that cost €15; the only difference being the label. Unfortunately, it is not uncommon for a child to refuse to go to school because they are being taunted over not having the right runners, etc. It can be useful to ask your child to do a little investigative reporting on the production of a particular item of clothing and then tell you about it. For instance where it is made, the pay and conditions for the workers, or what the carbon footprint is. If they discover things for themselves they are more likely to both understand and accept the information as interesting and useful.

BEING GOOD AT SPORTS OR OTHER ACTIVITIES

Whilst a bit of competitive spirit is healthy, it is good to encourage children to take part simply for the enjoyment of it. Both boys and girls can become more competitive in their teens but girls often lose interest in sports, particularly competitive sports, as they go through their teenage years. This is a phenomenon less common in boys, which may be partly due to the higher levels of testosterone being released and partly due to the 'top dog' syndrome. Anyone who has ever watched wildlife programmes will have seen lion cubs, young male primates and lots of other animals fighting to establish their position in the pack. Well, human beings aren't so different. Put a team of adolescent boys, or even post-adolescent boys, on a playing field and the old fight for supremacy is never far away. Testosterone is sometimes referred to as the aggression hormone, but it is also responsible for drive, energy, and so on. None of this is anything to be worried about but what is slightly concerning is the child who becomes angry or withdrawn, even lashing out at others, if they aren't a winner. As adults we should all be aware that losing is as important as winning when it comes to developing into a well-rounded person, but we have to remember to talk to our children about this, as they may not have come to that conclusion by themselves yet. Unfortunately, not all adults are aware of this. It never ceases to surprise me when standing at the sideline, when my grandson is playing GAA or soccer, the level of aggression in some of the parents, both in the way they shout 'encouragement' to their children and the way they sometimes react to other parents and even to match officials. Is it any wonder that some children cannot accept losing graciously?

This, of course, does not just apply to sport. It could involve other hobbies such as dancing, music, gymnastics or chess. Children love to talk about the medals or trophies they have won, which is understandable, and I accept that introducing competition to certain activities can encourage dedication and commitment, but they should also be taught to expect the odd failure and to be aware of the other person when they are the winner. Not succeeding or getting something wrong is a golden opportunity to improve. If they can look at what happened and what they might do differently next time the lesson is more valuable than any trophy that they win. Of course some girls can be every bit as competitive as boys and are frequently just as aggressive in their competitiveness. Even for girls who are not involved in sports they can be really competitive in areas such as academic ability, friendships, fashion sense or popularity. Again they sometimes need reminding that they do not always have to be the winner or the best.

POPULARITY

The human being is a pack animal so therefore it is normal for them to feel the need to belong and fit into at least one pack. Some children, however, go beyond this and are not happy with being a part of the pack; they have a desire or need to either be in control of the pack, or, at least, be one of the kingpins. Some children attain this quite naturally by having leadership qualities, and others work very hard at it. For girls this is often, but not always, a role filled by one of the prettier members of the group and for boys often, but not always, by a particularly sporty or strong boy. Being a leader is often a positive role but can at times verge on the negative.

If the leader of the group has qualities such as empathy and integrity, the group can often work really well and is usually inclusive and good-natured, but where the leader is lacking in these qualities, it can sometimes result in bullying, exclusion and elitism, and this, in turn, may lead to fairly damaging behaviour causing low self-esteem to not only other group members but also to anybody else who they do not deem to be worthy of membership.

The number of children who rate their popularity by the number of friends they have on social media or the number of 'likes' they get for a certain post is a worrying trend. I don't know about you but I have had only a handful of what I would call good friends throughout my life and I don't think that makes me particularly unpopular but children of this generation have an entirely different view of friendship. I believe it is good to challenge them when they talk about these virtual friends because I think if we don't we are going along with the designer trainer mentality which, as stated previously, is a myth built on superficiality. A couple of good conversations to have with your children when talking about friendship could involve some of the following questions:

- *How often do you see this friend?*
  If they have never seen this 'friend' face to face they are probably not really a friend. It doesn't mean that they need to stop contact but it is no harm to draw the distinction.
- *What have you got in common?*
  This hopefully will outline similarities and differences that you can draw them out on. It might also highlight any areas of concern.
- *Would you rely on them if you needed them?*
  As you know, a real friend is prepared to help out where possible, even if this is just to keep someone company and tell them things will be ok.
- *Could they rely on you if they needed you?*
  As above. This is related to empathy and our children need to be encouraged to be empathetic.

- *If they told you a secret would you keep it?*
  This is easier for some people than others, and I don't just mean children. Maybe you aren't great at this either. This is about trust and we all need to be able to trust our friends. As you know, trust is one of the elements that underpins all relationships so if our children learn to be trustworthy and expect trustworthiness in friends this will be second nature to them in adult relationships. I am sure you will agree that an adult relationship without trust is not a real relationship.
- *If they told you a secret that was potentially harmful to them or someone else what would you do?*
  This may seem to be a contradiction of the above but it is important for children to realise that if they have information regarding a friend (even a virtual friend) that might prevent harm coming to them, or somebody associated with them, the caring and responsible thing to do is to tell a trusted adult. This might be you but it is good to let our children know that it is ok if it isn't you. Sometimes it is easier for them to talk to somebody who isn't quite so close as a parent - possibly a grandparent, an older brother or sister, a teacher or a coach.

We should also try to encourage our children to enjoy their own company and not always look for reassurance from others. It can help them to develop a healthy sense of self-esteem and individuality, and if we do this they would be less likely to be concerned with the number of 'likes' they get on social media. Of course we want our children to have friends, and have the ability to mix with others and have fun, but they should also grow up with the knowledge that not everybody will like them and this is okay. After all, they will not like everybody they meet going through life either.

Frequently Identified Worries

4

Worries are different from the everyday pressures identified in Chapter 3. All children worry; in fact all people worry, some more than others. When children are given the opportunity to explore what worries them most they usually identify the following core worries:

- Body developments
- Secondary school
- Boyfriend/girlfriend issues
- Dying
- Parents dying
- Parents separating
- Violence
- Rape/assault
- Being homeless
- Drugs and drink

BODY DEVELOPMENTS

This worry centres around what pre-teens see happening with their bodies, what they are afraid of happening and what they are afraid of not happening. Chapters 5 and 11 may help you in addressing this.

SECONDARY SCHOOL

Sixth-class children are at one of the most important transitional periods of their lives. They have more than likely attended the same primary school since they were four or five and feel very comfortable with their friends, their teachers, the regime, etc. Then it is all change! They worry about practical things such as getting lost in a new school. Secondary schools are usually much larger than primary schools, with many more students, more classrooms, etc., so this worry is not completely unfounded. Reassure your child that they will be looked after in their new school, there is normally an orientation day and they will be given a plan of the school.

They frequently worry that they may become separated from the class during a change of lesson. A simple instruction, such as to follow the signs for reception and tell the secretary your class name or number and the lesson you should be in and she will tell you how to get there, is generally enough to reassure them.

They also worry about bullying by older children. They should be reassured that all schools should have an anti-bullying procedure in place but just remind them of the steps they should take if there is a problem. For instance, speak to their year head and if this does not have the desired effect speak to the principal. And always speak to you.

Another worry is that they may not struggle with new subjects or that there will be unmanageable amounts of homework. As adults you know that the first year in secondary school is as much an assessment year as anything else. One way to reassure them about this is to draw a comparison to them moving into sixth class from fifth class and ask them was the work instantly more difficult? Moving into first year from sixth class will be just the same. There is, generally speaking, not much more homework than in sixth class, with the exception of some subjects. Encourage them to plan out their homework timetable and not put off homework just because it isn't due in the next day.

Making new friends is more daunting to some than others; practical tips like how to start a conversation, smiling and reminding them that most people want to make friends should help.

Some children will instantly love secondary school, which is great; others, however, will not. I often used the following example, which children always found useful. When my son started secondary school he absolutely hated it. He would come out at the end of the day with a grey face and when asked how his day was he would invariably say 'crap'. There was no bullying and he was managing the work but he was not happy. He never liked change and this was at the root of his problem. We struck a deal that I would check in with him regularly and if he was not happy by the end of the second term I would arrange for him to go to the local school the following year. At the end of April I asked him what he wanted to do and he said even though he still didn't like it he didn't see the point in changing and having to get used to a new school so he decided to stay even though he would probably never like it. Well stay he did and by the time he graduated in sixth year he cried because he was so sad to be leaving. So the rule of thumb is to listen to the concern, let them know that you have heard them but try not to have a knee-jerk reaction. Both his sisters were perfectly happy when they went to secondary school but everybody is different and it is far from unusual for children to be resistant to change.

BOYFRIEND/GIRLFRIEND ISSUES

Not getting a boyfriend or girlfriend is linked to the pressure of fitting in. It might help to encourage your child to treat people well, be friendly and be open to new friendships whilst nurturing old ones. Remind them that there is no rush and when they feel ready if they need to talk you will be happy to listen.

DYING

This worry is linked to our being spiritual beings. There are not many people who have not had this worry when they have been unable to sleep at night. I think this is a gentle reminder that we should not ignore this part of our being. After all, you can be sure that if your dog is lying on their rug at night unable to sleep they are not lying there worrying about what happens to them when they die because they are not spiritual beings. It is very rarely a daytime worry or one that crops up when we are enjoying themselves. Whilst we can't promise our children that they won't die, what we can do is explain that this is their opportunity to check out how they are living their lives. For instance, they can ask themselves have they made somebody smile that day, or the opposite - have they made somebody sad; have they helped anybody; have they put the needs of somebody else in front of their own needs, etc.

Parents Dying

Again it would be lovely to reassure your child that this won't happen but that is not possible. It is good to encourage your children to be positive and celebrate the fact that it is because they love their parents that they worry about them not being there so they should take every opportunity they can to show this. Also, the fact is most children reach adulthood before they have to face this and this gives them a lot of comfort.

Parents Separating

Whilst it is true that some parents who argue eventually separate, it is certainly not always the case. Some parents are a lot more vocal in expressing their opinions and are not even necessarily aware that their heated discussions could be perceived as arguing by their children. A little reassurance might be helpful if this is the case.

Of course some parents will separate and where this is the case the child is sometimes concerned for their status. Will I still be cared for? By whom? Does this mean that I won't see my mother or father again? Am I still loved? And so on. This will be covered in more depth in Chapter 9 in the discussion on emotional development.

VIOLENCE

This is a mainly a worry for boys as they are more likely to be involved in physical fights than teenage girls. As parents we can give them skills to avoid violent confrontations such as avoiding situations where there is unruly behaviour associated with alcohol, teach them to read a situation and to remove themselves before it becomes violent, not to allow themselves to get dragged into a confrontation because they feel they need to save face, the importance of staying with their friends and looking out for each other, etc. Ask your children how they might recognise if a situation is becoming potentially dangerous. Talk to them about body language, raised voices, physical contact, somebody bumping into them or shoving them and pretending it is accidental just to get a response. Whilst we do not want to make our children overly fearful it will be useful for them to be aware of possible dangers.

RAPE/ASSAULT

This worry was more likely to come up in discussions if there had been a high-profile rape or assault case in the news. As adults it is quite frightening to think that there are people at large who behave in this way but as children you are even more vulnerable and therefore find it more frightening. We want our children to be safe and understand how to protect themselves but we also want to reassure them that generally the world is quite a safe place. I have lived in two major cities in my life and managed to get to my age (which is quite old) without being attacked. Having said this, being sensible and taking precautions is advisable so give your child common-sense instructions such as not separating themselves from friends when out, not taking shortcuts through deserted areas such as playing fields, school grounds, etc., keeping their parents informed of their whereabouts and not going off with people they don't know well, even if they are the same age. It is important, however, to remember that the majority of sexual violence perpetrated against children is done so by somebody known to them - a partner, friend or family member - and whilst we do not want to damage the bond between our children and those close to them they should all be aware of how to deal with situations that make them uncomfortable or worried in any way. This will be covered more comprehensively in Chapter 16.

BEING HOMELESS

We can't deny that there is a problem with homelessness in most major cities but the vast majority of us will not find ourselves a victim of this. Some homeless people have other underlying problems such as alcohol or drug abuse, mental illness or a culmination of these issues. Others may find themselves in a position where they have lost their homes due to unaffordable rents, either because of a personal crisis such as unemployment or illness, or even because of unreasonable rent increases by landlords. Whilst we cannot guarantee to our children that homelessness will never happen to them, it may help if we point out to them that a good education leading to a job that pays a decent wage will offer them some reassurance. Finally, even though hopefully it will never happen to them, they should be encouraged to have empathy for people in this position and help whenever they can.

DRUGS AND DRINK

You only have to take a walk through the centre of most cities to see that there is a problem with alcohol and drug abuse. The important thing for our children is to identify that they have a choice. As parents if you want to broach the subject you can ask them what they think the first drug of choice is. The answer to this is probably tobacco and alcohol. If we decide we are not going to smoke or drink alcohol because of the ill effect on our health we are much less likely to use other drugs. That of course is not to say that everybody who smokes or drinks alcohol is more likely to be a drug user, but there is a certain safety in not being prepared to use any substance that will damage your health. Quite a difficult conversation if you are a smoker or somebody who drinks yourself. You can still have the conversation though, pointing out how hard you find it to stop smoking and stressing the dangers of abusing alcohol.

Some children unfortunately come from families where alcohol is a problem and this can quite naturally have the effect of making them more than a little fearful of it and may stop them from ever drinking alcohol as adults, but even children who do not have this problem in their family will more than likely have observed somebody under the influence and it can be quite scary for them. In my experience though, most children say that they probably will drink when they are older and some of them even think it is quite amusing to see people drunk. I would encourage them not to drink until they are legally old enough to buy it for themselves and then restrict it to social occasions and remember it is a really dangerous drug if abused. Explain that the reason there is a legal age for purchasing alcohol is because it is a toxic substance that can cause problems to the developing brain. You may find it useful to visit www.drinkaware.ie, where you will find a really informative leaflet on this topic.

* * *

Finally, it is good to finish on a positive so remind your child that everybody worries to some extent as this is the way we have evolved to keep ourselves safe. After all, if we never worried and threw caution to the wind we would put ourselves in unnecessary danger. It only becomes a problem if it stops you from living your life as normal. So the main thing they need to remember is to talk to you or somebody else if there is something on their mind. A worry frequently grows out of control when we try to hide it but when we talk about it with somebody else it starts to shrink and hopefully may even vanish altogether.

'The Talk'

One thing that has definitely not changed since I was an adolescent is the embarrassment with some children, particularly girls, regarding THE TALK. People think that because there are frequent advertisements on the television for pads or tampons that this probably makes it easier for girls to talk to their parents about menstruating, but this is not always the case. It is far from unusual for girls to dread getting their first period because they will have to tell someone and they don't want to say the word.

Earlier in the book I asked you to think back to how your sexual development was handled. Do you have good memories of this part of your development or, like me, are they just shrouded in embarrassment? So many of my peers have very similar stories and even now when speaking to groups of parents they are more likely to have had a negative than a positive experience in relation to how this issue was handled in their families.

See does this strike a chord with you: I was the youngest of four girls born and brought up in an averagely dysfunctional family in Liverpool. I understood what periods were due to lots of hushed conversations between friends who 'had come on' as the term was then. I thought the day would never come when mine would start. This was, and is, a very exciting time for most girls; it is confirmation that you are moving out of childhood and into the next phase and that your development is on track. There are, of course, some girls who do not welcome this at all and indeed some can be quite scared or upset at the prospect. I, however, was not one of these. When the day finally came, mixed with the excitement was the growing concern that I would have to utter the dreaded word 'period' to my mother. I thought she may get a fit of the vapours or something, or I might get into trouble for saying a dirty word because this was not a word that had ever been uttered in front of me at home. I decided to plead ignorance and just said that I had blood in my pants. My mother's reply was 'oh that's just your period. All your sisters have them. I'll get you some pads', which she did, and the only instruction she gave me when handing them over was 'don't let your father see them.' I was never quite sure whether she thought he would be envious or maybe he would rob them. That was the one and only conversation – if you can call it a conversation – that I had with my mother about my sexual development. This does not mean that she was a bad mother or that she didn't care for me; she was doing the best she could with a subject that made her very uncomfortable because of her upbringing, which was loving in some ways but certainly did not involve much, if any, openness about sexual development. Sound familiar? Don't worry; if it does you are in good company!

The important thing is what we take away from these experiences. For me, it was the determination that I would do my best to be open and positive about this aspect of my daughters' lives. The last thing I would have wanted for them was to feel shame or embarrassment, which are the two overriding emotions I remember from my own experience.

Being open and comfortable with your children is obviously the ideal but it is not the only indication of good parenting. There is probably more damage done by parents who feel they 'should' be having 'the talk' with their children when they would really rather do anything but. Although my experience was far from ideal, I'm not sure that I would have liked my mother to be any more explicit than she was. I would probably have found it excruciatingly embarrassing.

If you feel that you would like to broach the subject with your daughter it might be best done in a conversational way. Start by talking about what life was like for you at her age, including the embarrassing bits and the bits you wished had been handled differently. Talk openly about your PMS if you have it, explaining that it is uncomfortable but will pass. Try not to overdramatise it and don't feel the need to conceal packets of pads or tampons from the male members of the family. Just leave them with all other toiletries in the bathroom cupboard and if asked about them by either your son or daughter answer truthfully. Unlike my sister, who panicked when her son came downstairs with a tampon out of the packet and asked her what it was and instead of the truth she told him that they were stoppers for wine bottles. I do hope he managed to work it out for himself later in life or it could lead to some very embarrassing dinner conversations if a previously opened bottle of wine with a tampon in it was produced! Or the mother who told me that she told her son that they were for his sister's art project and when his friend came over to play she found them drawing eyes on them and pretending they were mice.

So, what can you say if you are asked by a child what they are for? Very simply, tell the truth. Simple language is best so say something like 'They are for when I have a period.' They may then ask 'what is that' so you can go on to say 'once a month my body prepares itself for pregnancy by making a new lining in my womb and if I don't need the lining it breaks away and comes out of my vagina.' If you are asked where the vagina is just explain that it is an opening between your legs. You are answering their questions as they ask them and not assuming that you have to give all of the information at once. They will probably have lost interest before you get to the part regarding the whereabouts of the vagina and be more interested in when dinner will be ready but they will realise that you answered their question honestly and although they may not have fully understood everything they will be aware that you told them the truth and this will encourage them to come back another time if they have other questions.

Just be careful when you are answering a child's questions that you are sure you have heard the question as they intended it. The problem is that we hear children's questions with adults' ears. I was told by a woman at a parent talk that her eight-year-old daughter had asked her what sex was. She was immediately thrown into the quandary of how to answer this, so she said 'well, sex can mean gender, being male or female.' The child said 'no, I don't think that's it' so she went on to say that sex is something that mummies and daddies do to make babies, to which the child said 'well you know when I shouted for you before why did you say that you would just be a couple of secs?' So remember, less is more.

When it comes to adolescent boys, they are often completely overlooked as far as talking to them about their sexual development. Unlike our daughters, they do not need bras or pads. The most they will ever need is deodorant, hair gel and eventually razors. It is a good idea for fathers or a father figure to be involved at this point if at all possible and I would suggest that they talk about their own development as opposed to the child's development. If there is no father or father figure available of course the mum can answer any questions that are likely to be asked as long as she is prepared with the necessary information, which can be gleaned at the touch of a button from good old Google. When talking to your son about this it is best to use the same approach as previously mentioned and make it as conversational as possible, remembering that our sons' feelings can be every bit as fragile as our daughters'. Talk about how you felt when your body started to develop, try to remember some of the questions you would have liked to ask and if you have some funny stories it might help them to relax. We do not always have to tell the truth; you can create a story about your childhood that will illustrate a point you want to make.

One thing to be careful of is not to use a question as an opportunity to impress the child with your vast array of knowledge. Sometimes parents do this because they feel they may never get another opportunity to explain something that they consider to be important. This is not usually the case though; in fact the opposite is probably true. If you labour the point using 100 words instead of 10 they are less likely to ask you any questions going forward. For instance, my husband's area of expertise when the children were younger was geography and if they ever asked him a question about geography a vast array of atlases would be produced and a lengthy lecture would follow, all of this delivered to children with decidedly glazed-over expressions. They eventually stopped asking; I think they preferred to get the answer wrong than to have to suffer the lecture. And not one of them did Leaving Cert Geography.

My husband is far from the only parent guilty of this though. Maybe you recognise yourself? I once had a twelve-year-old boy in a group I was working with who expressed a wide and varied knowledge on the subject of sexuality. So much so that I had to ask him to stop interrupting so the other children would not hear anything inappropriate, and I promised to talk to him after the workshop. I asked him how he knew as much as he did and he said 'My dad told me. I just asked him does sex hurt and he told me loads of other stuff.' He laughed and said despite his mum's objections his dad kept going, saying 'he has to know sometime' and 'it's all only natural'. The dad was well-meaning and the child obviously listened because he was able to feedback most of what he'd heard to me, albeit without much real understanding. He actually did not need to know most of it, however, and possibly would be reluctant to ask anything else in the future in case he lost another hour of his life to a lecture. So remember there is a fine line between answering a question truthfully and going into overkill.

Technology

I am frequently asked if I have observed any great change in the behaviour of children since I started working in this field. Well the answer is for the most part no, or at least not hugely. The perception is that children are much more sexually aware now than when their parents were children. Although this may be the case with some, it is not necessarily so with all children. Whilst it is true that some children have access to more information, and sometimes this information is inappropriate for their age group, not all children fall into this category and many children will maintain their innocence for most of their childhood. Having said this, there are significant numbers of children who are handed a loaded gun without any supervision at all. The loaded gun I refer to is technology in the form of smartphones or other internet-enabled devices. I have lost count of the number of times I have arrived at a school to be told that there has been a problem with somebody inappropriately using a phone in school or somebody being the victim of cyberbullying. I think as parents we have a duty to supervise the use of technology and television where our children are involved. This, however, is becoming increasingly more difficult with the availability of smartphones and other portable devices. Parents can come under pressure from children to allow them to have the latest gadget and because they love them and don't want them to feel alienated from their peer group the temptation is to give into the pressure and buy them the very thing that may eventually cause them harm. This harm can come in a number of forms: cyber bullying, a subject which appears in the news far too frequently; pornography, which they can access at the press of a button; online gaming; and the more insidious problem of breakdown in communication.

Most children are curious and that includes sexual curiosity. I can certainly remember as a child looking up words like 'sex' and 'penis' in the dictionary, and it is this same curiosity that sometimes drives our children to access some of the more harmful sites available on the internet or to watch certain programmes that are not designed for their age group. If you discover your child has accessed one of these sites don't overreact. Talk to them calmly about your concern that they have seen something not meant for their age group. Explain that the reason there is an 18 Cert on some things is because it has been decided by experts that some of the content in these films/posts/chat rooms, etc. can be harmful to children and young people because they often portray confusing ideas about sex and where it belongs in everyday life and relationships, and ask them is there anything that has worried them or they want to talk about in respect of what they have seen.

Unfortunately, even those children closely monitored at home can have second-hand access to inappropriate information by way of friends or other children in the school who are not monitored as closely. As parents you must decide whether or not you are happy with your child having unsupervised access to the internet and at what age you are happy for them to have a mobile phone. Some children will be very responsible in their use of technology but there will always be some who are less responsible. It doesn't make them bad children, just curious ones, and unfortunately curiosity without responsible input can be harmful. Of course it isn't just the use of phones or other devices that can be harmful. Occasionally when viewing television with your children a topic that you would deem inappropriate may crop up, even before the watershed at times, but at least if you are there you can give them factual information in a respectful way, whereas the child who habitually secretly watches pornography is possibly in danger of developing an unhealthy attitude to sex. At this impressionable time in their life constant viewing of sexually explicit material can encourage the misunderstanding that all adult relationships are based primarily on sexual activity instead of mutual love and respect, fun, etc. It is therefore good practice for them to leave their phones, tablets, etc. downstairs when they go to bed. They may be resistant to this suggestion but it is one area where I believe parents should stand firm and eventually when they see that you are not open to negotiation on this point they will come to accept it.

Most schools and many parents have been faced with the necessity of addressing the issue of cyberbullying. It is a good idea to open up a conversation with your child regarding this even if there has been no incidence of it. Ask them what they understand by the term and you may find they can educate you. Use simple questions like:

- Why do you think it happens?
- Would you know what to do if it happened to you?
- What would you do if you became aware it was happening to somebody else?

Educate yourself about the law surrounding this and how to deal with it should it occur and if you are comfortable with your child using social media you should have access to their account.

Another aspect of technology that is causing concern amongst parents is the amount of time some children spend gaming online. I meet children in schools who can hardly keep their eyes open because they continue playing video games into the night when their parents think they are safely sound asleep, with some of them spending more than four hours at a time in front of a screen. I know that some parents may say 'well at least they are safe and I know where they are', but are they safe and do you know where they are? Maybe physically, but a lot of parents are not aware that a number of the games that are played online include interaction with other gamers. These may be other children known to your child but in some cases they are complete strangers and not always children. Of course we do not need to police every aspect of our child's life – that would stifle their independence – but we do have a duty as parents to keep them safe or as safe as possible.

I think it is safe to say that the cat is very definitely out of the bag as far as children and technology is concerned and nobody is ever going to successfully put it back in the bag, even if they wanted to. So do we refuse to allow our children to watch television or own a mobile phone or any other technological device? I don't think this is very likely either. What we can do, though, is to firstly set restrictions on the amount of time the child or young person spends online, with very clear penalties if this agreement is broken. Secondly, have a reasonable discussion with them about why you are doing this. It is important that they understand your concerns and I mean *really* understand them so that going forward, when it becomes more difficult for you to impose restrictions, they are more likely to self-monitor their behaviour.

Online games in themselves are not a problem; I know a large number of adults who get great enjoyment from playing them and some of them are really inventive and thought-provoking, but the phenomenon of gaming addiction is becoming increasingly more commonplace. Of course not every child who enjoys playing video games is in danger of becoming addicted. But for those who do it may result in them becoming withdrawn, uncommunicative, unmotivated and disinterested in any other activities. They can even become aggressive when they are forced to stop playing for dinner, homework, etc. I have spoken to some children who have admitted to hitting a parent or smashing a control because they became so angry at being interrupted. So if you have noticed a marked change in the behaviour of your child that is associated with the amount of time spent online it would be a good idea to start imposing restrictions and possibly seeking help from your family doctor if there are real concerns.

In order for parents to handle the situation of phone/ technology use it is worthwhile for them to honestly examine their own phone use as children frequently take their lead from us. All too often I have seen parents sitting in a park or other public places with their child totally ignoring them and at best answering them in monosyllables when the child is doing their best to engage them in conversation, or parents pushing a child along in a buggy with a phone attached to their ear or their earphones in instead of chatting to the child. The superficial chat between a parent and a baby or toddler is so important. Just pointing out things like buses or dogs, or even making eye contact with them, is the basis for future communication.

This point was illustrated very clearly recently when I went out for an early dinner with my husband to a local restaurant and a young couple arrived with a child who was probably about four or five years old. They sat down and the first thing they did was hand him an iPad and take out their phones. Nobody said a word until the waiter came to take their order, they then said a few words to each other between scrolling through their phones but neither of them attempted to engage the child in conversation the whole time they were there. What a waste of an opportunity! It made me quite sad. On the surface they were having a pleasant meal out and the child was physically cared for and having nice food bought for him, but what about his emotional well-being? If we saw parents with a child in a restaurant buying food for themselves but leaving the child without any we would quite rightly be horrified but while this child was not being deprived of a physical need he was most definitely being deprived of an emotional connection. So as I said, before we restrict our child's use of technology we need to honestly assess our own and ask ourselves how often during the day has it interfered with a real-life conversation with one of our children, or anybody else for that matter?

Another danger with children overusing technology in general, but particularly playing video games with violent content, is the impact on their ability to empathise. Let me be clear here. I am not suggesting that every child who watches

online videos or enjoys playing computerised games is a socio-
path, but when we see news items about somebody being
beaten up or humiliated whilst somebody else films it and
then posts it on social media we have to question the effect not
only on young minds but on not-so-young minds also. The
message that is being sent out here is that it is ok to enjoy
somebody else's pain. Frankly I find this terrifying.

This was brought home to me a few years ago when my
grandson, who was six years old at the time, came home from
school and said that there was a girl in his class who cried a
lot and one of the boys told him and some others that he was
going to bring his iPad into school the next day, make her cry,
video it and post it online. Naturally both his mother and I
were horrified and asked him what he did when he heard this.
He said 'I kind of laughed'; when asked why he said he didn't
know. On further discussion he said he did know it was wrong
and he felt sorry for the girl but didn't really know what to say,
and this from a child who is actively encouraged to be empathetic and has a naturally gentle nature. So you can see that it
is not as straightforward as we may think. There are, however,
homes where empathy has less importance and children from
these homes may be the very ones who become involved in
more serious behaviour as they get older. It probably helps to
ask your children what they think someone else is feeling in
a given situation and if they display a lack of empathy, as we
all do at times, maybe draw their attention to this. The bottom
line of this story is that he was encouraged to do the right
thing so the next day he told the teacher about the conversation and it was dealt with and hopefully lessons were learnt.
You can be sure the child involved was not evil but he may
possibly have had older siblings who, like a lot of teenagers,
watch shaming videos online and who may not always be too
mindful about the impact should these be viewed by a younger
brother or sister.

Sexual Curiosity

Sexual curiosity is perfectly normal in children but unfortunately I occasionally come into contact with children who have started acting out of this normal curiosity and are already experimenting sexually. This is obviously both shocking and sad when a child as young as eleven or twelve has decided for whatever reason that this behaviour is 'normal' for them. Sometimes it is inappropriate touching or oral sex but can result in full sexual intercourse for some children. There are a number of contributing factors at play when this happens. It could be a lack of parental involvement or other family problems, and particularly for girls low self-esteem often resulting from neglect, emotional abuse, etc. Even though they understand on some level that this behaviour is not healthy they may feel that at least they are getting the attention that they often crave but are being denied in their homes. They are usually involved in this kind of behaviour with other children of similar age but not always. Occasionally there is an older child or even an adult involved. Obviously the latter is more serious. Although sexual activity between children is still against the law, where this activity involves a much older child or an adult this is a far more serious crime and will be dealt with accordingly.

Of course there are those children who just have a very real curiosity about their and others' bodies, more specifically the genital area. Games of doctors and nurses have been played for as long as there have been real doctors and nurses. So don't confuse this natural curiosity among children with actual sexual activity. 'I'll show you mine if you show me yours' is a normal game amongst children and one that most of us have played at some time and usually without any ill effect. I clearly remember playing this game when I was about four years old with a boy who was roughly the same age. We lived on the same street and his mum was friendly with my mum. We were playing in the back yard and he showed me his penis and demonstrated how he could 'wee' up against the wall. That was the first penis I had ever seen and I was not overly impressed; neither was I upset in any way by it. I did, however, decline to show him mine, which on reflection was probably a bit sly. From what I remember he took this in his stride and didn't seem overly bothered, and I think we went on doing whatever else we were doing before the excursion into the biology lesson. Children generally do not put too much pass on these things and they are really just one of many rites of passage. However, if my mother had ventured into the yard at that moment I can guarantee that there would have been a very large mountain made of a very small molehill and I would probably have ended up with a much more negative memory of the incident than I did. It was another four or five years before myself and my cousins compared genitals, from what I remember in quite an academic way, but nothing that could be considered as sexual activity. So, as I said, natural curiosity is a normal part of childhood and not to be compared with childhood sexual activity.

If children ask questions of a sexual nature it can sometimes shock or worry parents and I have been approached on a number of occasions by anxious mums who feel that they may have bungled a reply to one of these questions. We all know that as parents we can sometimes be taken off-guard and this can cause us to say the wrong thing or at least not say the right thing. So if your child unexpectedly asks a question that you consider inappropriate or even just a bit embarrassing for you to answer play for time so that you can think about what you want to say; maybe just say, 'oh good question; I am just going to the bathroom so we will have a chat when I come back.' I have had a number of examples of children asking questions in class that have taken me by surprise but the vast majority of them were really useful and the whole class learnt something from one child's curiosity and openness. A perfect example of this was a fifth-class girl who asked 'why do I get tickles down there when I see people kissing on the telly?' The other girls in the class all laughed hysterically and expressed shock at her saying something like this, but I explained that that part of the body has lots of nerve endings and it is normal to feel tickles there when you are reacting to something exciting like somebody kissing romantically on the television, or even playing hide and seek or chasing. When I explained this a number of other girls agreed that they had felt this sensation also but they thought it was too 'dirty' to ask about. By answering this question in this way it not only gave them an explanation about what was happening it also hopefully encouraged them to think about this part of their body in a less shameful way.

What has not changed since I was this age is the readiness in some boys to admit to some level of sexual activity. This may just be 'meeting' (which is the terminology generally used by children when talking about romantic kissing) or they may also occasionally talk about exploring their own bodies, resulting in masturbation. Of course this is not true of all boys and many eleven- and twelve-year-old boys are still totally impervious to all things sexual. Girls can be more secretive and would very rarely talk about masturbating or exploring their bodies in any way. This does not mean that they don't do it because of course some do, but they are much more likely to keep this to themselves and may not even talk about this with friends.

Girls often opt to talk about 'a girl I know'. It is always worth listening to these stories, even when you suspect a deal of exaggeration. When I'm told a story about 'a girl I know' who may be acting in a sexually precocious manner, for instance participating in sexual touching with boys, I usually throw this open for discussion with the group and ask them what they think is going on, what they might be able to say to this girl to change her behaviour and why do they think she behaves in this way. As parents you can do something similar if you are told something by your child that concerns you. It is far more productive than demonising the person they are talking about. Just to say something like 'what do you think of that behaviour?' can open up dialogue between parent and child and encourage the child to express their opinion, which is something we as parents don't always do. I have been guilty on more than one occasion of reacting to something that one of my children told me with a lecture on the evils of a particular type of behaviour only to kick myself later for not just listening and asking them their opinion. As parents we are sometimes afraid that we haven't made our position or thoughts on a particular subject crystal clear. Well we usually have! What isn't always crystal clear however is what our children actually think about a particular behaviour. So park the lecture and ask questions rather than issue warnings. If your children are anything like mine they become warning deaf!

Working with a group of children in a classroom setting is of course much different from the relationship between parent and child. There is occasionally more honesty because it can be less embarrassing to speak to a stranger and there is also the opportunity for children to write anonymous questions which does not happen in the home. Sometimes though, it is little more than instinct that a child is behaving dangerously or inappropriately, maybe somebody becoming uncomfortable or knowing glances passing between children. However, there are very definite red lights such as the girl who looks for reassurance that you cannot get pregnant until your periods have started and becomes distressed when you tell her that this is not always strictly accurate, or the girl who wants to know if you can get pregnant by swallowing sperm. The best I can do for these children in the short time that I spend with them is to reinforce their uniqueness, try to get through to them that as human beings they deserve to be treated with respect, love and kindness, and give them the skills to say 'no'; and where an actual disclosure is made ensure that they get the help they need. As parents we are unlikely to address these points with our children and most children are equally unlikely to address them with us. There are children though who have less of a filter and may feel comfortable to ask these kinds of questions at home. It may just be something they have heard in school or out on the road or it could be an actual worry. You have to decide how you want to handle this – as I have said you are the expert on your child – but it might help if you just ask them why they are asking the question, give them an accurate but brief reply (no overkill of information, remember this is child's question heard with adult ears) and maintain a poker face. It will not help if you become angry at language used or go into Miss Marple mode and get the spotlight out. If you overreact they will just avoid asking any similar questions again. As I said earlier, children behaving in this way are the exception rather than the rule so please don't run away with the idea that this behaviour is commonplace. Thankfully the nearest most twelve-year-olds get to sexual behaviour is the odd kiss.

Intellectual Development

You're Not the Boss of Me!

It is important when looking at adolescent development that we look at the whole person and not just concentrate on physical development, as so often happens. People develop roughly speaking in four ways: intellectually, emotionally, spiritually and physically. It is sometimes easier to concentrate on the physical developments because we can see what is happening to the body and if we need an answer we can get this at the touch of a button, but I believe it is a mistake to overemphasise this part of our child's development. Granted, a lot of the questions that our children may have are related to body developments because there are things that they may have to deal with - such as periods or breast development or previously non-existent pubic hair - but we shouldn't ignore the other areas that are developing at the same time.

A child's intellectual development is related in a large part to decision-making, the connection between action and consequence, and helping them to develop negotiating skills. For parents who have an adolescent in their family for the first time it can feel like a hand grenade has been thrown into the centre of family life. They may feel as if someone has replaced their loving, smiling, enthusiastic child with a snarling, sulky and argumentative facsimile, and that's on a good day! Well let's try and get all of this into perspective. When your child appears to be oppositional for the sake of it they are often trying to tell you 'You're not the boss of me' and 'I can think this one out for myself'. Of course you still are the boss of them but we do have to start relinquishing some of our control at this stage. Their job is to push away at the boundaries that we have put in place and our job as parents is to stop them gaining ground too quickly. So what I would suggest is give and take. As the child gets older encourage them to do more for themselves and be more responsible. When this happens we can reward them by loosening the reins and giving them more freedom. If you think about this for a minute, just imagine if they never pushed but remained happy for us to make all their decisions for them, never challenged, always behaved like responsible human beings - how worried would you be? I know personally I would be completely freaked out. I would be very concerned that they had no drive, initiative or sense of fun and I would probably be waiting for them to morph into a serial killer and be tempted to remove all sharp objects from view. Now put the boot on the other foot: if you acquiesce to every new request without reservation they would be equally freaked out. Parents and children have an understanding of each other's roles without ever verbalising them. Often the battle is as important as the request and winning the occasional victory gives them the sense of freedom and responsibility that they are desperately seeking.

I'M NOT EVERYBODY ELSE'S PARENT!

Most children happily admit to being cheeky and arguing with their parents at times. When asked what they argue most about at home it is usually not getting their own way or being wrongly accused of something. So let's look at the first point. Your child makes a request to go somewhere or do something that they have not previously been allowed do. There are three possible responses to the request:

- Yes of course you can.
- No you can't!
- Give me more details before I decide.

They will of course usually be delighted with the first response, but not always. Sometimes when we receive a request from our children they are secretly hoping we might refuse. This happens when they themselves are a bit nervous about the planned activity. They may have made plans with their friends and on one hand love the idea of what is planned but on the other hand not feel entirely comfortable with the planned activity. Their request to us can sometimes be their way of establishing the safety or appropriateness of what is planned. If you say 'yes' then you obviously think it is safe and if you say 'no' the reverse is true. This does not mean that they will take a negative response from you without an argument. Even though they might be secretly pleased that you are denying the request they will still object, sometimes most vociferously because they feel they should.

The second response is almost positive to elicit an argument from them. I am sure that the majority of you already familiar with the script for these arguments.

Child: Can I go to town with Emma on Saturday?

Parent: No you can't.

Child: Why? Everybody else in my class has been going to town for the past year. All of their parents think it is okay.

Parent: I don't care who else is allowed; I'm not everybody else's parent.

Child: You're just trying to ruin my life; you never let me do anything! I'll end up with no friends because of you! Just tell me why I can't go.

Parent: Because I said so!

Child: I hate you!!!

Child usually exits stage left at this point, slamming the door on their way out, and stomps upstairs to their room to cry very loudly in the hope that you will feel sorry enough for them to give in. Sometimes this works because most parents just want their children to be happy and popular and we can't bear to think of them being unhappy and losing out on friendships because of us. Alternatively, you stick to your guns and totally ignore the histrionics, knowing that sooner or later they will get bored in their bedroom and come downstairs - usually when they get hungry.

Now let's examine the third response. Sometimes this is our first reaction and sometimes this comes after the histrionics. There are a number of benefits to this response.

- Obviously you are in a better position to make a judgement when you have all available information.
- If you are not happy with the plans you can now negotiate.
- Even if you have no intention of giving permission you are at least showing them that you are willing to listen and you are interested in what they have to say.

So the bottom line is ask for all of the details, look like you're considering it and then say 'no' if you are still not comfortable with the request.

One of the things that children find most annoying about parents is their refusal to explain their decisions, especially when they respond to their request for an explanation with the phrase 'because I say so'. Can you remember being a child yourself and having this said to you? It used to drive me mad! Sometimes this is the response of a tired adult who just doesn't feel like getting into a big argument, or it could just be a knee-jerk reaction, more instinctive than thought through. These instinctive responses may be due to the fact that your son or daughter has asked to do something that you were not allowed to do when you were a child and your automatic response can be to say 'no' without consideration. I think you will agree that it is a response that we would probably never use when speaking to anybody other than our children. When children are asked what they would like to happen instead of

this, without exception they say they would like an explanation. Even as a child I could never understand why children
are sometimes treated with less courtesy than is afforded to
adults. Lead by example; it will lay down good foundations for
future dialogue, especially when your children are teenagers
and you may be looking for explanations from them about
their behaviour.

Even if you are not prepared to negotiate with your children
on a certain point it can be a useful exercise for you to understand exactly why you are denying a request. Don't just do this
superficially; look at it as an academic exercise and argue the
child's case with yourself. You may be surprised at how many
of the rules we lay down are simply because they were rules for
us when we were growing up. I'm not suggesting that this is
enough reason to change them but neither is it enough reason
to uphold them.

Another main bone of contention with children is when
they are accused of doing something that they haven't done.
Parents are fallible and not the all-seeing eye, a fact they often
try to hide from their children. They may sometimes assume
they know what has happened and prejudge a situation
without having all the facts, which is often a recipe for disaster.
Even when you are tired and have heard the same argument
from the same children a hundred times before try to get all
of the facts before making a judgement because, as you know,
the role of protagonist can change and we should resist the
temptation of allotting this role to the same suspect every
time. Just because the child was guilty of a certain behaviour
yesterday and maybe the day before it doesn't always follow
that the same child is guilty today. Always allow the opportunity for them to give their version of events and then leave
space for reasonable doubt. As those of you with more than
one child know, a lot of arguments that occur emanate from
disagreements between siblings. These arguments are not
only normal, they are a necessary part of our childhood development. We obviously don't want our children beating each
other up but neither should we expect them to get on with each
other all of the time. Encourage them to solve disagreements

for themselves if at all possible, especially if they are more or less a similar age. This will be a useful skill for them going forward. If you feel the need to get involved maybe ask them both to think about what part they played in the argument and how their actions may have contributed to the disagreement, then encourage them to apologise and learn from this going forward. I know this sounds a bit like *The Waltons* and not always possible to achieve, especially if we are tired ourselves, but if we at least try to adopt this stance on as many occasions as we reasonably can I promise it will have a positive impact.

We should resist apportioning labels to our children, even if they are positive labels, such as gifted, kind, pretty or friendly. It is best to commend an action, for instance 'that was a really kind thing you did.' Equally, children should never have negative labels attached to them, such as aggressive, liar or lazy, as this can become a self-fulfilling prophecy. As a child I was the 'cheeky' one and frequently found myself being chastised for saying something or doing something that my older sister may have also said or done but because she was the 'quiet' one she got away with it scot free. I can still get annoyed about the injustice of this now. Maybe I should get out more!

A useful exercise can be to ask yourself what label, if any, was allotted to you as a child and what effect did it have on you, both then and as an adult. Then ask yourself have you labelled any of your children, and with what label or labels, why did this happen and can you see any effect from this now or any possible effect going forward? If you can see a negative effect from labelling one thing you can do to counteract this is to insert a positive affirmation where a negative label has been used in the past. So for instance, with the child who is labelled as lazy praise them when they are even slightly industrious. You may find that they will try to live up to this praise rather than being resigned to being lazy. For the child who is labelled as a liar (a particularly harmful label in my opinion) tell them you believe them as often as possible and congratulate them for telling the truth, especially when it means that the truth has a negative impact on them. This hopefully will be useful going forward into their teens when trust is essential. If they get used to not being believed they may just decide that there is no point in being truthful anyway and become more accomplished liars, which is not only damaging for the parent–child relationship but it also has a negative impact on the child's future relationships. Children who are perceived as being cheeky are often also quick-thinking and articulate, and some of them have a highly developed sense of justice, which I am sure you will agree are all positive attributes; however they can be prone to impetuosity. So with this in mind it may be useful to congratulate the child for their bravery in speaking their mind, but remind them that it is far more effective when done politely, especially when speaking to an adult. Finally, encourage them to think before they speak and think of the effect of what they are going to say both on themselves and the recipient of their opinion.

RESPECT THEIR OPINIONS

Children can become quite frustrated and angry when they are not treated with the same respect as expected by adults. This probably happens more frequently than we realise and for a variety of reasons, some of them more valid than others. Thankfully, most of us have left the old maxim 'children should be seen and not heard' behind but as adults we can show flagrant disregard for children's opinions or feelings at times. It is of course understandable that a busy parent or teacher may sometimes have to make an executive decision. That comes with the territory. I do however think it is useful and good modelling for all adults to take the opinions and feelings of children into consideration as often as possible. There are a number of memories from my childhood of when I felt disrespected or overlooked but thankfully there are other memories when the opposite happened. One occasion was when my dad asked me what colour I thought he should paint the paving in the garden that he had just laid. I said pink, my favourite colour at the time. He did it! I felt so special that I had been listened to. It looked awful and I am sure he hated it but he obviously thought it was worth having a bit of an eyesore to make me happy. I also acutely remember the total opposite happening. On this occasion, I went to the corner shop to buy a bar of chocolate on my way back to school after lunch. The owner of the shop was an elderly lady who was a friend of my grandmother. I arrived at the shop and another customer was being served; I waited my turn and was just about to say what I wanted when a number of women from a nearby factory came in and I was told to wait until they had been served. I was quite annoyed that the fact that I was next was disregarded so I said to my friend 'come on Vivienne, I'm not waiting here!', left the shop and went to school. On returning home from school both my mother and grandmother were waiting for me with a less than welcoming reception. I was asked why I had been so cheeky to my grandmother's friend, who had apparently told them that I had stormed out of the shop because she served the factory girls first because they had to get back to work. I was incredulous. I explained that I was going back to school and I would have been late if I had waited for all of them to be served. I stated that I had just as much right as they had to be served and steadfastly refused to offer an apology. My mother did not try to force me as she had done on other occasions so I can only conclude that although she may not have wholeheartedly agreed with me she did understand my point of view. Of course you may disagree entirely and think it was unacceptable behaviour but by not being overly chastised for this personality trait I developed into an adult who is not afraid to speak my mind both for my benefit and that of others who may find it more difficult to do so. Surely respect should not be graded, as in one person deserves more than another person; everyone deserves respect irrespective of age, social class, profession, etc.

Another very important point about intellectual development is the importance of encouraging autonomy and independence. Sometimes as parents who love our children we are inclined to do things for them that they could very well do for themselves. This is not doing them any favours. It is not just the practical things like teaching them to tie their own laces or learning to dress themselves, although these are an important start, but also things such as allowing them to order for themselves in restaurants or to seek assistance in shops if needed. I heard a father in a bookshop very recently talking to his daughter as they were looking for a particular book that they could not find; he said to the daughter 'go and ask the assistant have they got it.' She was really reluctant and said 'no I don't want to, you ask'; he eventually persuaded her to ask the assistant when it would have undoubtedly been easier and quicker for him to just give in and ask himself. This encouragement resulted in her taking responsibility for herself, thus increasing her self-confidence. Maybe next time you are out for a family meal get your child to give their own order to the waiter and deal with any questions regarding this that the waiter may ask. Obviously if they order filet mignon you may have to step in, otherwise leave them to it.

Emotional Development

9

Emotional development is about more than mood swings and temper tantrums. It is about emotional maturity, the growing sense of individuality and the way we look at things from an emotional perspective. It is also connected with the ability to empathise, to look beyond the superficial and attraction to another person. It is around this age that children often take on causes. This is associated with empathy; they become more aware of injustice and have a better understanding of how others may be feeling, or at least most of them do. Usually at this age we start to realise that all that glisters is not gold. We recognise personality types and are attracted to some more than others. We also start to look more closely at our own motivations, the effect we have on others and the effect they have on us.

There is not an adult alive who did not experience mood swings during adolescence, admittedly some more than others, and for some these mood swings continue into adult life and can continue to be affected by hormones. Some children can be born with a propensity to moodiness, it is just a part of their personality, but this is quite different to the moodiness that can develop due to hormonal changes during puberty. They can go from being a perfectly happy ray of sunshine to morose and difficult within minutes. They may cry at the drop of a hat for no apparent reason or have flashes of anger that may even result in them throwing things or punching a door or wall. I remember one of my children crying while watching an advertisement on the television and when I asked her why she was crying she insisted that the advertisement was the saddest thing she had ever seen. Of course she wasn't really crying because of the advertisement, it was merely that her emotions were barely concealed beneath the surface so anything could have made her cry; tears of happiness, sadness or anger and frustration are never far away with most children going through adolescence. They frequently don't know why they are crying; sometimes a real sense of melancholy descends on them and it can be quite frightening when this happens because they don't understand why they feel like this or if they are going to feel like this forever. This is commonly referred to as a mood swing. They are a well-documented side effect of puberty, not very pleasant for the onlooker or the child but nothing to be concerned about unless they are causing distress or harm to themselves, the people around them or their surroundings. It ceases to be a mood swing if the child is routinely in a black mood and becomes withdrawn and their usual default personality does not resurface. In these circum-stances it is always advisable to seek medical help. It is more than likely just the effect of the shift in hormones which will become less dramatic over time but in some cases there could be other underlying causes which would require treatment. So the usual rule of thumb applies: when in doubt ask for advice.

A little visit down memory lane might help you understand what is happening with your child at this point in their life. Try to remember how you dealt with worries, disappointments, rejection, uncertainty, attraction, etc. and see if there is any similarity in your child's responses to these things.

I would not have said I was a particularly moody child but I can very clearly remember times when I felt all around me was quite bleak. I understand now that this was a hormonal shift but back then I just thought I was having the worst possible life. I particularly remember when I was about eleven years old I went to spend the night with my eldest sister, who had recently married. As I was lying in bed finding it hard to go asleep one of these hormonal mood swings descended on me and I started to cry; she heard me and came into the bedroom to see what was wrong. I didn't really know why I was crying but not wanting to sound weird I told her that I was crying because she didn't live at home anymore. She was very moved by this and promised to take me shopping the next day. She told all of the family how sensitive I was and how attached I was to her. This event went down in family folklore. I *was* quite attached to her as it happened but that certainly was not why I was crying. I was crying because I felt really miserable for no particular reason that I could identify, probably made worse by the fact that it was late August and the thought of returning to school in September did not have me exactly cock-a-hoop. Children often feel that they are the only ones experiencing these feelings and need reassurance that they are not going mad.

ARGUMENTS

Arguments with parents and brothers and sisters frequently become more common at this time and occasionally these arguments with siblings can even become physical, especially where there are two or more children in the family who are undergoing these hormonal changes. It is slightly more common for boys rather than girls to have sudden spurts of anger and throw things or punch doors or physically lash out but girls can also become instantly and unreasonably angry, even lashing out at people for no apparent reason. Whilst parents quite naturally do not want their children to be violent or aggressive I would not get too worried about this. Of course you should have a talk to them about their unacceptable and possibly dangerous behaviour, explaining to them as simply as possible why it is happening, but I wouldn't be threatening them with an ASBO just yet. Trust me, more children than not admit to succumbing to these rages.

Of course not all boys experience more aggressive behaviour going through adolescence; there are some boys who seem to make the transition into adulthood quite seamlessly and slip under the radar completely. However, my observation from working with children is that a higher percentage of boys than girls will experience these flashes of anger. This is partly due to the rising levels of testosterone, sometimes referred to as the aggression hormone. It is not purely attributed to this though. There are also other factors at play such as a less developed emotional vocabulary in some boys and the fact that they may show less willingness than their sisters to talk about their problems or worries. I would even go so far as to suggest that for some boys there is a difficulty in their actual ability to identify what they are worried about, which in turn can make them moody or withdrawn and angry at times. Again this is not all boys; some boys are very open to engaging on this level and some girls are less open. This is not a hard fact but an observation based on many years of working with children and teenagers. If you notice your son becoming moody or more aggressive it would do no harm to let him know that you have observed this and ask if there is anything worrying or upsetting him. It might be a good idea to also explain that sometimes there does not have to be an actual problem, it could just be a mood swing because some boys are under the impression that only girls fall victim to mood swings. They can be inclined to think of hormones as a 'female problem'.

EXPRESSING FEELINGS

As parents we have to be careful about gender stereotypes. For instance, we may use different vocabulary and even tones of voice when speaking to a male or female child. We may encourage more aggressive, ambitious or even ruthless behaviour in boys whilst encouraging more caring, gentle and sensitive behaviour in girls. You may have dismissed this possibility already but I would ask you to very honestly play the video in your head of how you relate to your son and daughter and ask yourself are there differences and if there are why this is so. If there is no difference in the way you communicate with your son and daughter that's great, but if you do feel that these differences are present do not worry. I am not suggesting that you alter the way you talk to your children or need to think about everything you say before you say it to ensure total equality and political correctness, but even the slightest adjustment can bring about positive changes. For instance, if you get the chance praise caring behaviour in boys and men and praise ambition and drive in girls and women. The most useful and permanent changes come about from mirroring behaviour. If our children observe both parents being kind and not afraid to show emotion and ask for help it will be more natural for them to also do this. Equally, if both parents display drive, ambition and strength of character children will not just attribute these qualities to one sex or the other.

During my work with children I often ask them if in their opinion boys and girls have the same feelings. Their most common response is that girls have a lot more feelings than boys. Of course what they mean by this is that girls generally talk more about their feelings and express feelings that some boys may try to hide. For instance, girls are more likely on the whole to outwardly express sadness or hurt by crying or sad facial expressions than boys, who frequently attempt to hide these emotions. Both sexes are, however, equally comfortable to express feelings of happiness, anger or excitement. By the age of ten or eleven years old some boys already have the belief that it is not masculine or even unsafe to show feelings of hurt or to appear worried. They believe that a boy should be able to 'handle things'; they shouldn't need to ask for help and above all they should never look weak. I don't think these assumptions are necessarily passed on by parents, or at least most parents, so where do they get them from? The answer to that is probably everywhere: media, advertising, history books, industry, commerce, etc., etc. The type of male who is held up as an example to aspire to is often the successful politician, sportsman or captain of industry, the Alan Sugar figure whose very fame is built on his ruthlessness and single-mindedness. Of course these qualities are also present in some successful women but we only have to look at the fact that there are more women than men in the caring professions and fewer in top roles in business or industry to see that these traits are both more commonly displayed and generally more valued in men than women. As previously stated, a good way to redress this situation is to mirror the qualities that you would like your children to develop. There is nothing at all wrong with encouraging our sons to be capable, strong, ambitious, etc., but we should also encourage them not to be afraid to ask for help and to let them know it is perfectly okay for them to cry if they are sad, to encourage empathy and integrity, to treat others with kindness and love, and expect to receive the same. In short, speak to them the way we would speak to our daughters! Boys and girls, men and women are different with their own natural strengths and if we acknowledge these differences and work on developing the qualities that we admire together it may make talking easier for children and adults alike.

For those of you reading this who have daughters you will probably already have realised that the majority of girls from the age of about four years old love playing relationship games. Of course they don't know they are playing relationship games; they think they are playing make believe, such as mummies and daddies, school, doctors and nurses, etc. These games help them to develop an emotional vocabulary, which is maybe one of the reasons why a lot of girls, and women, are more comfortable talking about their emotions than most boys or men. If a group of female friends get together they will more than likely discuss relationships, absent friends, families, etc. This may be loosely termed as gossip, some of which is very superficial and occasionally unkind, but it can also be very therapeutic. On the other hand, a group of male friends are far more likely to discuss sport, work, money, politics, etc., or report facts of one kind or another. It is less likely that they will talk on a personal level about problems or worries or other people. Obviously this observation does not apply to everyone but the general consensus is that it is fairly accurate a lot of the time. Which is a shame because the old expression 'a problem shared is a problem halved' is very often true and in general women are more likely to share a problem than men.

BITCHINESS

Another observation made by children is that 'girls are bitchier than boys' - an observation that is not necessarily accurate. I have met some girls who could be accurately described in this way but I have also met some boys of whom this description would be fairly accurate. Boys often get quite frustrated with girls for 'the way they carry on an argument' or 'try to get everyone else involved'. This may be stereotyping but there is some evidence to suggest that it may be true to some extent. However, to say that boys are not guilty of the same behaviour would be untrue. There has been research of late that would suggest that both sexes are capable of this behaviour. Boys are generally more likely to offend with the use of insults or spreading rumours whereas girls may use more subtle methods such as exclusion or wrapping insults in sugary language. Girls often preface an insult with 'no offense but' whilst being fully aware that what they are about to say is offensive; yet they justify the insult by saying that they did not mean any offense. Growing up, my mother, like lots of others, said, 'If you can't say anything nice don't say anything at all.' Well it is as true today as it was then. We should encourage our children to treat others with respect and expect the same in return. We as adults should resist using insulting language when having conversations about people we may not like as this sends the message to our children that it is acceptable to speak to and about people in this way. It is perfectly normal that we do not like everybody and for our children to be aware of this, but it is not okay for them to think that this gives us permission to be insulting or offensive.

ROMANTIC INTEREST

The other obvious emotional development that occurs at this time is the newfound interest in the opposite gender, or for some the same gender. Many eleven- or twelve-year-olds might have little or no romantic interest, which is perfectly normal, but there are others who definitely will to some extent, which is also perfectly normal. It is quite common for eleven-/ twelve-year-old girls to spend a lot of their time together talking about boys; most boys on the other hand spend less time talking about girls and more time talking about sport or their favourite television programme. They do talk about girls but not to the same extent as girls talk about boys.

Many parents get a little worried when their children start showing signs of romantic interest and they may actively discourage it or even try to forbid it. I understand that this reaction is out of concern but it is not always helpful. If parents overreact it may just encourage children to become more secretive. I'm not suggesting that they should be encouraged to go out on intimate little dinner dates but it might be a good idea to encourage them to talk about their newfound interest. So try not to panic. They have either become or are about to become fertile and with this there is an awakening of sexual interest. This is all perfectly normal, with some young people showing more interest than others. Some parents take all of this in their stride but for some it can cause sleepless nights. If you are the latter and feel the need to approach the subject it might be useful to explain to your child what is happening to their body and subsequently their feelings. Reassure them that it is okay for them to 'like' somebody in this way but these feelings are adult feelings and as they are still children it would be best if they just enjoyed the feelings for the moment and resisted the urge, if they have it, to act on them. Even when they do act on these feelings it is rarely more than just kissing and frequently as part of a game involving friends such as spin the bottle - a game that I and most other adults enjoyed in their youth without coming to any harm.

Of course some restrictions can not only be helpful but necessary and as long as you have a good explanation for the child as to why these restrictions are in place they can usually see the relevance of them and in fact are often pleased that they have obvious boundaries to push against.

A number of years ago I was asked to address the issue of dating and romantic relationships with a sixth class in a co-educational school as there had been a fairly serious incident between a boy and girl who were both twelve years old at the time. Apparently these two children had become an 'item' in September after returning to school following the summer break. All was going well and both sets of parents seemed to be quite happy with the 'relationship', even allowing them to go on dates together and spend quite a bit of time in each other's company to the exclusion of other friends. By the end of the first term in school the boy had decided that he didn't want to continue the relationship and 'broke up' with the girl. To say that she took this break-up extremely seriously is an understatement. She refused to eat, get out of bed or go back to school after the Christmas break. She eventually had to be referred by her GP for psychiatric help. The boy, on returning to school, was harangued almost daily by the girls in the class for breaking their friend's heart. Luckily, the severity of the reaction in this instant is the exception rather than the rule, but I have frequently spoken to young people, usually but not solely girls, who have been upset by the ending of a relationship.

The main difference in this case was the apparent blessing of both sets of parents, which gave their children the message that this kind of relationship at their age was both accept-able and normal. Whilst I do not recommend an autocratic approach I do think that there was a lack of appropriate guidance and boundaries put in place by both sets of parents in this case. It might have been advisable for these parents to acknowledge that they understand that these two children liked each other in a romantic way but to explain that these feelings are adult feelings and acting on them would not be a good idea for the time being. They could have also had more encouragement to maintain their other friendships and told if they wanted to go to the cinema or for a burger with each other it should be done in the company of other children too. I understand that by saying this there would not necessarily be any guarantee that the children in question would listen but at least in this scenario the parents would not be giving a romantic relationship their blessing and their reservations would be made clear to both parties. Allowing children of this age to conduct a romantic relationship could be compared to allowing a three-year-old to go out to play on the road. They may think this would be fun but it could be unsafe and would quite possibly result in them being harmed.

If your child is displaying worrying or precocious behaviour regarding relationships and you want to address it the following tips may be useful:

- Get as many facts as you can before speaking to them.
- Stay calm and talk *to them not at them*.
- Pick your moment – not around the dinner table or in front of other family members.
- Do not use your lecture voice.
- Tell them the facts as you understand them and state why you are worried.
- Ask them for their opinion and input.
- Do not threaten, especially with idle threats such as grounding them until they are eighteen. Of course you may feel the need to impose rules or restrictions but if so try to be as reasonable as possible whilst being firm.
- Try to reach a compromise as this will involve the child in taking responsibility on some level.
- Be clear about the consequences of not sticking to the agreement.

Finally, I don't think it helps to make sexual curiosity shameful; it is not only quite healthy and normal but an exciting part of growing up. If as parents we can explain our reservations or worries in a rational way we have a far better chance of opening up healthy dialogue with our children, which will be very useful going forward. Autocratic parenting and threats of grounding carry much less weight when they are teenagers!

PHYSICAL CONTACT

I think a lot of parents would be surprised at how much physical contact actually happens between boys and girls of this age. By this I mean harmless physical contact such as hugging, linking arms and holding hands. Most girls take for granted that they will both give and receive hugs from family members or friends or both but this is not always the case with boys. Very rarely do I observe boys hugging each other, other than a man hug as way of celebrating a goal in a match or some other sporting event. They do, however, frequently give and receive hugs from female friends or the girls in their class if they happen to go to a co-educational school. Boys often make the observation that hugging makes them feel calm. It is really important that we continue to hug our sons as well as our daughters during and after puberty. It is comforting for boys and parents and it encourages them to be gentle and caring. Sometimes boys feel that they should not be hugging or kissing parents after a certain age, which is not only sad but some research would say unhealthy. They frequently look to parents for validation of their feelings in this situation and parents, sensing some resistance, may stop offering hugs or kisses as they don't want to embarrass them, particularly in front of friends. So now we have the situation of the child and the parents probably both wanting a hug but not quite knowing if it is acceptable to look for one.

A number of years ago, whilst discussing this topic with a group of trainee facilitators one of them said that she still hugged and kissed her daughter who was eleven years old but that her ten-year-old son did not want to be hugged. Not wanting to challenge anyone's parenting skills, I said that she knew her child best and left it at that. When this same facilitator returned the following week for another training session she said that she had conducted a little experiment with her son as follows: she brought her son and daughter to the cinema and whilst watching the film she lifted her son's hand, put it on the armrest of the seat and started stroking it. After a minute or so she stopped and returned her hand to her lap. Her son then picked up her hand and placed it back on top of his so that she could continue to stroke it. She also said that since this incident he was now being far more demonstrative with his feelings, freely giving hugs and insisting on sitting next to her whilst watching television and placing her arm around his shoulders. She was pleasantly surprised as, like most parents, she enjoyed showing affection to both her children but mistakenly assumed that her son no longer wanted it when in fact it was she who was afraid of forcing unwanted contact which in turn led him to believe he shouldn't be looking for it. If as parents we continue to be openly affectionate with our children it will not become an issue irrespective of age or gender.

CONSENT

Talking to children about consent is something that both parents and some teachers are reluctant to do. I can totally understand this because when we think of consent we think of agreeing to sexual activity and quite rightly this has no place in a child's life. That is why I have purposely included the topic at this point in the book and not in the discussion about sexual curiosity.

Consent can be talked about without any reference to sex at all and can be introduced at any age using appropriate examples. The following are a list of suggestions that you might find useful:

- You can remind your children that before entering the bedroom of a sibling they should look for permission or consent.
- If they ask permission to go somewhere or do something make sure to use the word 'consent' as well as 'permission'.
- Talk about personal space. Most parents have been subjected to their children fighting in the back of the car. It normally goes something like 'Mum, his leg is touching mine!' Or 'Tell X to move to their own space!' Or even, 'Mum tell Y to stop looking out of my window!' These are all perfect examples of not invading someone's personal space.
- Remind your child not to just take a pencil, etc. from a classmate's desk without their consent.

Most schools nowadays have Stay Safe programmes where things like 'good touch' and 'bad touch' are discussed but at home we don't always want to address the issue quite as formally, which is why the above examples might come in useful.

Consent is about rights, permission, agreement, consideration, and respect, which are not just the preserve of adults. Another way we can make this more valid and clear for a child is for us as parents to respect their privacy and personal space. As soon as a child starts to intimate that they are uncomfortable undressing in front of us or locking the bathroom door it is a signal that they need their privacy. Some parents are very open when it comes to nudity and have no problem with open bathroom doors or changing in front of family members, or anybody else for that matter, but just because one person is comfortable with this it does not always follow that everybody else is and we need to be sensitive to the feelings of others, especially adolescent children who are frequently very body-conscious and easily embarrassed so the last thing they want is for anybody to see their developing body or for them to see their parents' bodies. I am not sure which of these things offends them most but I do know both get a very emphatic reaction when raised in class.

Finally, a child should never be forced to display physical affection, as in hugs and kisses, if they don't want to. As children we always kissed our parents goodnight before going to bed; nothing at all wrong with this - it's a tradition that I continued with my own family and in fact still do even though my children are all grown. I do, however, remember being distinctly uncomfortable as a child if certain relatives were in the house at bedtime and my mum insisted that I gave them a kiss as well. Kissing should be for close family and only when the child does so spontaneously, likewise we should never assume as adults that a child would be comfortable to sit on our knee. In short, we should give children the same if not more consideration than adults in this respect.

I am not suggesting that you tie yourself up with rules and regulations and a lot of parents are already dealing with the subject satisfactorily, so the bottom line, as with most things, is common sense and a little bit of forward planning. Hopefully by the time your children are teenagers it will be less of an issue than it seems to be now.

LGBTQ+ CHILDREN

Between the ages of eleven to thirteen years is when a lot of children first question their sexuality and if they are being brought up in a house where there is dismissive or disrespectful language used when talking about sexuality or gender this can make it very difficult for them to either accept who they are or to talk to their parents about their worries. Just imagine how difficult it must be for the child in this position hearing derogatory comments about sexuality or gender from the very people they need to confide in. Is it any wonder that some children decide to hide how they feel out of fear of rejection?

Even if your child is not gay you have a responsibility to the child in their class who is. Ask yourself how you would feel if it were your child. It is an unfortunate fact that homophobic bullying still happens, less often it is true but even one incident of it is one too many. Much of it goes unreported by the victim because they may feel if they make a fuss it could get worse or they may feel that nothing would be done anyway. All schools should have an anti-bullying strategy and this is usually posted on the school website but you can ask the principal for a copy if it isn't. Whether bullying is as a result of race, sexuality, gender, religion, class, etc. it really doesn't matter - it is all wrong. There are a couple of things we as parents can do to help combat it, whether it applies to one of our children or not:

- Ask your child do they know what the anti-bullying strategy is in their school.
- Do they think that students are influenced by it?
- Have they observed bullying, particularly on grounds of sexuality or gender?
- What form did it take?

- Was it reported?
- What action was taken?
- Did they do anything to help?
- What would they have liked to happen if it were them being bullied?
- Why do they think that people sometimes get bullied because of these issues?

When addressing sexuality with children in this age group I often found it useful to use a visual aid such as pie chart. I would explain to the group that this pie chart is made up of elements of our everyday life as a person, such as school, family time, friendships, sport and eating, leaving one section blank, I point out that other than this one section - which I would then fill in with the word 'attraction' - there is absolutely no difference between a gay person and a straight person. A gay person does not wake up in the morning and think 'yes, still gay' any more than a straight person wakes up and thinks 'yes, still straight'. They may be sporty, they may not; they may be artistic, they may not; they may be fun, they may not; they may be nice, they may not. It is just who we are - no more, no less - and it should be no more interesting than this.

Surely it should be far more important to us as parents that our children grow up with the ability to love another human being and be capable of displaying empathy and integrity rather than to be concerned with the gender of the person they find attractive. The awakening of sexual attraction at this age is normal; for some that attraction will be for somebody of the opposite gender and for others for somebody of the same gender and it should not be viewed as a problem to be dealt with. This is just who your child is; they are not broken so therefore they do not need fixing.

Because most parents are in heterosexual relationships they do not always have the background knowledge to understand same-sex attraction or gender issues and this can make them a bit nervous about saying the wrong thing. If this is the case you can get support from a number of organisations, such as BelongTo and TENI. BelongTo is for LGBTQ+ young people between the ages of fourteen and twenty-three and TENI is the Transgender Equality Network of Ireland. Both of these organisations will offer practical advice to both the young person themselves and their parents.

Gender and sexuality are completely different, with issues related to gender often being more complex and harder for people to understand. There is still the assumption among some people that it is a matter of choice and that parents should not pander to the whims of the child who says that their physical body does not accurately reflect their gender. There is also quite a lot of misunderstanding about hormone therapy and puberty blockers, with some people getting quite incensed at the notion of a parent allowing children as young as ten years of age to access this therapy. Puberty blockers will halt the development of puberty in the child until they are old enough to pursue treatment; they will not cause the child to develop physical characteristics of the opposite sex. I don't think this is a decision that any parent takes lightly and neither is it the first course of action recommended by the medical profession, but I think it is fair to say that by the time a parent has reached the point of accessing help they have had years of dealing with a confused and frequently unhappy child and it is not, as some people believe, a knee-jerk reaction to a little girl not wanting to wear a dress or a little boy wanting to play with dolls instead of a football.

After delivering a talk for parents a couple of years ago I had the privilege of talking to a mum who gave me great insight into the challenges of being the parent of a transgender child and what everyday life was like for her son. On the evening in question I was approached by a woman who said that she wanted to talk to me about her child who was in fifth class and would be participating in an RSE workshop delivered by my team the following week. She said that her 'daughter' Emma* would from the next day be officially known by the name Darragh,* and she didn't know if attending the

---

* Names have been altered in the interests of confidentiality.

workshop was a good idea. She told me that the school was being very supportive and she was going to meet the parents of Darragh's friends to explain the situation to them the next day. She said that he was due to start on puberty blockers over the next few weeks but as luck would have it menstruation had already started the day before I spoke to her. This really upset the child, who flatly refused to believe it was a period and insisted that it was just a cut. I asked when it became apparent there was an issue with gender and she said it was there from day one. The child had always insisted he was a boy and flatly refused to wear girl's clothes; the mother thought this was just your average tomboy behaviour and didn't worry too much about it.

It came to a head when the time came for Emma to make her First Holy Communion. Naturally enough, the mum planned a shopping trip to buy her dress and veil but the child became hysterical, saying 'I can't wear a dress, I'm a boy; everyone will laugh at me.' They eventually struck a bargain that the dress would be worn in the church and then it would be taken off, never to be worn again. The mum said she has never seen such a sad little child as in those communion photos. She vowed that was the last time that she would ever try to insist on anything like that. It was then that she decided to look for help. She said it hadn't been easy for her or her other children and she knew that there would be other hurdles ahead but she knew they had made the right decision.

One of the hardest things for this mum was grieving the loss of her little girl but she said it was made worthwhile by the obvious happiness of her little boy. When I hear people suggesting that this is a lifestyle choice it really makes me quite frustrated. I don't believe any parent would put themselves, their child or their family through this lightly. Would you? Move forward a couple of years and I am delighted to say that the last I heard Darragh is doing well. The school handled the transition wonderfully, as did Darragh's friends and the other children in the class. I generally find children are far more accepting of situations like this than many adults.

Gender issues are not as rare as they once were and some schools have more than one child in fifth or sixth class transitioning so if your child has questions or as a parent you feel you would like to address this yourself, Darragh's story could be a good example to use. Ask your child what they think Darragh was feeling on the day of the First Holy Communion or ask your son how he would feel if you made him wear a dress in front of the whole school (particularly a white one with a veil)? It might help them to understand some of the emotions experienced by Darragh at this time. It might also be useful to ask yourself how would you feel as a parent? What would you do? How would you want people to react?

IMPACT OF PARENTAL ARGUMENTS AND/OR SEPARATION

Another aspect of family life that children identify as a worry is their parents divorcing or separating. When I was young this was not as much of an option as it is today, whereas now most children will know somebody who is either divorced or separated. This can sometimes make them anxious, particularly when they hear their parents arguing. Let's face it, most couples argue occasionally and some more than others. It might not be too serious in the parents' eyes but to their children, who may be aware that their friends' parents have recently separated, it could possibly be really worrying. Things can appear to be very black and white through the eyes of a child. I can certainly remember feeling that my family was definitely the best family ever and I can also remember feeling that they were the worst. Children may sometimes measure the success and happiness of their family against information they are being fed by television programmes where the families they are observing either don't argue at all, have lots of good clean fun, and live in perfectly clean and tidy homes, or where the opposite is true and parents are seen to be abusive, disloyal and get divorced as easily as changing a library book. As adults we know that these extremes are for the entertainment of viewers and most of us accept it as just that, but it can be slightly different for children. The information they absorb is more inclined to be regurgitated, discussed with friends and occasionally used as a comparison for their life. I am not suggesting that you stop them watching soaps if they enjoy them, but it might be a good idea to be there for at least some of the viewing to add some balanced commentary. This helps to teach them to be discerning and to question other information going forward.

What was your family life like? If you have a minute try to picture the average day with your family of origin. What beliefs, expectations, worries and values did you take from this time? Like a lot of other people I was raised in an environment where people argued a lot. Myself and my sisters argued with each other and with our parents, mainly my mother, and my parents argued with each other. It was a very noisy house and not always pleasant. Due to rows and sulks and people falling out with other family members there were days when it was not the happiest place to be, but on other days it was the best place in the world. Sometimes when visiting friends I would witness their families behaving in a much more civilised manner with the whole family peacefully watching television, maybe their parents would be laughing and joking, and I used to think that it was only my family that argued. Of course when my friends came into my house there would be a very similar scene with all hostilities suspended until they left. We see our own family warts and all whereas we only see other families on their best behaviour. As adults we are of course aware of this but this is a revelation to children, who are far more likely to take things at face value. Children need to be told that arguments are a normal part of life and that adults don't always get on; it is good for children to witness the making-up process and to see their parents apologising when they have been in the wrong. It can be just as harmful for our children to never witness an argument as to constantly be rowing in front of them. If a child grows up without witnessing conflict it can occasionally create problems for them as adults if they have to deal with conflict in their relationships.

At this stage of your child's emotional development it can feel that life is one big battle. Your home can seem like a war zone on some days. At least mine did, with children arguing with each other and all of them arguing with me, which sometimes caused friction between myself and my husband. There were times when I felt like running away. When you are in the middle of a situation like this it can be very hard for you to see a way out or to even remember what life was like pre-adolescence (theirs not yours). Well, let me first of all reassure you that the vast majority of parents have felt like this at times. The trick is not to let arguing become a habit so that we snap at them because of their previous behaviour and they then fight back so we end up with this vicious circle of arguments and hysteria. It might be useful for you to think back to how arguments were dealt with in your house when you were this age: were you cheeky or would that have not been allowed? What did you argue about mostly and how were they resolved? As parents we often have that little niggle that says we must maintain control and win at all costs (or is that just me?). This is such a pressure to put on yourself so stop doing it. The first time I admitted to being wrong in an argument involving one of my children was not easy but after apologising I was surprised at how liberating it felt. Up to that point I had always tried to justify my behaviour or decisions, even if I was not totally convinced I was right myself, and it was very freeing to just be human and admit to a mistake instead of being 'Supermum'. The other benefit of doing this is that you are modelling good conflict management and this in turn may make it easier for our children to reflect on their behaviour and admit when they are wrong or even apologise at times (don't hold your breath though). There are no perfect parents or perfect children, and being prepared to admit to our imperfections as parents or children is as near to perfect as we can hope to get.

If we listen to our children without always trying to fix things they are more likely to talk to us honestly. Because we want our children to be happy we are sometimes inclined to minimise their problems; this can be as much for our sake as theirs. For instance if a child were to say they were worried about not getting a boyfriend or girlfriend when they are older it may inspire us as parents to reply 'don't be silly, you'll have loads of people interested in you.' There is nothing really wrong with this reply but what it could do is close down further comment from your child. If they have a particular worry, maybe about their appearance or possibly about shyness issues, they are much less likely to open up after they have been told not to be silly. It would be more helpful to say to the child 'why would you think that?' Listen to what they say without comment; if there is a problem talk about it and examine solutions together. Of course it is only natural that we would want to tell our child that we think they are wonderful and any prospective boyfriend or girlfriend would be lucky to have them, but we do also need to instil in our adolescent children the understanding that not everybody they meet will love them and that is ok, just as they will not love everybody they meet. We should also teach them that they do not need a romantic partner to be happy or complete.

A few rules of thumb that I collected on my way through parenthood are:

- Don't pay too much, if any, attention to the parent at the school gate who wants to tell you how perfect their child is.
- Don't judge your child's behaviour by the behaviour of their friends or compare them favourably or otherwise with these same friends. Remember how their friends behave when you are not around will be very different.
- Don't overreact if you find them out in a lie. All teenagers lie at times. (I was particularly inventive as a teenager.)
- Don't panic, you are not losing them but the more tightly you hold onto the reins the more they will struggle to get free.
- Try to enjoy them, don't take them too seriously and don't take yourself too seriously.

Spiritual Development

10

Spiritual development is a tricky subject, and one that gets very little attention usually. So what does it mean? What it is *not* is anything to do with religion. You can be any religion or no religion and still be spiritual. Equally, you can be a very religious person and totally out of touch spiritually.

I like to think that spiritual growth is best achieved by creating some level of happiness in the lives of those around us – both in our families and in the stranger who may cross your path any day of the week. Don't get me wrong, I am certainly not Mother Teresa, as anybody who knows me will testify to, but I do try to think the best of people and on a good day will usually bring a smile to somebody's face.

If you want to explore this topic with your children try to do it in a practical way. For instance:

- Encourage them to help others when they can – give them some ideas and ask them for theirs.
- Don't hurt people's feelings – we should never knowingly hurt somebody. I encounter some children who are of the belief that as long as they are being honest it is ok to say the most hurtful of things to someone.

- Do not be afraid to stand up and be counted - don't be a sheep, be a shepherd. Just because your friends might not like a person that doesn't mean you have to dislike them to.
- Encourage them to make someone smile every day. That person should be someone other than a friend.

Children are very receptive to 'vibes'. We learn to ignore them more and more the older we get but a child instinctively knows when somebody likes them; they also know when they are being put down. They might not always totally understand at the time but they just have a feeling of negativity when talking to some people. Try to connect with a time when you may have picked up either a good or bad vibe as a child - someone making you feel good about yourself or the opposite without the specific use of words.

A particular incident stands out for me when I was about eight years old. I remember a much older girl saying 'no offense but you should go to bed earlier because you have dark circles under your eyes.' She made it sound like she was saying this out of concern and then went on to continue a fairly pleasant conversation. I couldn't understand why I felt both embarrassed and hurt because I knew I had dark circles (a family trait) and she had smiled and said 'no offense' after all; her voice wasn't raised so I didn't really know whether I should be insulted or not. It was later disclosed to me by another girl who had been present at the time that the first girl didn't like me because she thought I was 'posh' (don't ask me why, we both lived in the same council estate) and she was actually jealous because my dad had recently acquired a second-hand and very old pink Studebaker (a very flash American car). We didn't keep it as it happened, on my mother's insistence and much to my father's chagrin, but us having the car obviously upset her as much as it upset my dad having to part with it. So you see, I knew I wasn't liked and was being insulted but I didn't really understand why. The opposite of this encounter is also worth pointing out. There are people in my life who always make me feel better. This doesn't mean they massage my ego or even put themselves out to be nice to me – it might just be an encounter at the shops – but I know when I walk away from that person that they like me and this makes me feel good and I assume makes them feel good also.

I really believe we get a number of opportunities throughout our lives to develop spiritually and if we ignore more of these opportunities than we take I think we are in danger of growing into fairly miserable and often lonely adults. By encouraging our children to be inclusive, not to hurt people's feelings and to be prepared to stand up and be counted we are giving them a very valuable gift for the future. Remember the old expression 'what goes around comes around'? There's more truth in this than one might initially think. If we give out positivity and happiness we are far more likely to attract the same back. By encouraging our children to be positive and see the best in people it is also helping to build their self-esteem.

Some people prefer to think of all of the above as being empathetic instead of spiritual and I am happy with that if you prefer to think of it in this way. The important thing is that we display kindness and understanding as often as possible.

Not all children are naturally empathetic and it is a quality that we as parents need to nurture. I have witnessed remarkable examples of children showing a distinct lack of empathy and happily I have also witnessed the opposite. One example is something I witnessed a couple of years ago in Dublin city centre.

It was a busy Saturday morning and as usual amongst the crowds of shoppers there were homeless people begging. One such man was sitting on the ground outside of a shop and nearby there was a group of women chatting. As I approached I noticed a little girl who was about four years old approaching the man on the ground; she stroked his head and asked him was he alright. His face lit up and and he told her he was and winked at her. She continued to stand next to him as if she was on guard duty with her hand on his head until her mum noticed and led her away. That may have been the only positive human contact that man had received in a long time and probably meant so much more to him than all of the coins that may be dropped silently into his waiting cup. Not only did it touch me, it made me feel more than slightly guilty because where I saw someone begging to whom I would have given money she saw a man in need of kindness and showed it to him completely unselfconsciously.

The following are a couple of points that you may find useful when talking to your children about this subject:

- Are you inclusive? How do you know? If you are not too bothered about inclusivity you may be less likely to notice or even care if your children don't exhibit this quality.
- Do you judge people on things like status, wealth or lack of, gender, sexuality, race, religion or accent? If you do your children are more likely to make similar judgements.
- Do you do your best to treat others how you would like to be treated? We often pay lip service to this and there are not many people who would own up to not doing it, but it can sometimes be quite challenging to do this in practice because most of us are, after all, more concerned with our own comfort and wellbeing than that of others.
- Do you actively encourage your children to do the same? The best way to do this is by example but we should also remind them when necessary to ask themselves 'how would I want to be treated if that were me?'

Finally, we should never start any conversation with 'no offense but ...' because what we are actually saying when we do this is 'I am just about to offend you and I don't want you to get annoyed when I do.' We should also remind our children that this is unacceptable. Some of the most hurtful things I have heard have been prefaced with this. Sometimes children justify using this expression because they are, in their words, 'just being honest'. Well sometimes it is far better not to be. As I was taught from a very young age, 'if you haven't got anything nice to say don't say anything at all.'

Physical
Development

11

So to the part that some parents seem to find most awkward to talk about. As I mentioned, I am a parent so can therefore entirely understand this awkwardness, and I want to reassure you that it is perfectly normal. I am not suggesting that this should stop you having a conversation but don't be too hard on yourself if you find it difficult and try to remember that if you are feeling awkward your child is probably feeling more awkward so keep checking in with them that they are happy to continue.

I have spoken to thousands of parents over the years and most of them feel that they would like to be able to talk to their children/adolescents about their body developments or at least be able to answer their questions should they come up. So what I will attempt to do here is to give you the confidence to deal with any queries that your children may throw at you.

I am not going to make this chapter technical as there are any number of excellent books on sale that will give you biological and factual information and I would suggest that if you are unsure of how the body works then maybe a good place to start would be with one of these books. Just don't try to impart all of your newfound knowledge on your children; believe me they won't want it or thank you for it.

GIRLS' DEVELOPMENT

Let's start with girls' development. The hormones involved in physical development for girls are oestrogen and progesterone; they are produced in the ovaries which are small glands situated in the lower abdomen just in front of the hip bones. The normal age range for physical development in girls is between ten and sixteen years of age. The most usual age range for the first signs of puberty is between eleven and thirteen years. However, if your child shows signs of developing before this or has not started to menstruate by the age of seventeen do not panic. As with everything else in life there are always exceptions to the rule, but if you are concerned you should consult your doctor. Below we discuss the signs to look out for.

Vaginal Discharge

This can happen well in advance of the first period, for some as long as two years before the first period while for others only a matter of months. Discharge is the way the vagina keeps itself clean. You can explain to your daughter that it will be present for the rest of her life or at least up to the menopause[†] and that at certain times of the month (when ovulating[‡]) the discharge will become heavier and of a runnier consistency. Once discharge appears personal hygiene becomes even more important so explain how to keep this area of the body clean. Some children are quite shocked when I explain that they need to wash inside the lips (labia) surrounding the vagina as this

---

[†]   If your child asks what is the menopause just explain that when women reach their mid-forties or thereabouts their hormones start to decrease and eventually their period will stop, which means that they are no longer fertile and therefore unable to have any more children.
[‡]   This usually occurs midway between periods, when an egg is being released from her ovary.

is where discharge, sweat, urine and menstrual blood collects and can cause an unpleasant odour if not dealt with daily.

Breast Development

Some girls seemingly appear to sprout breasts almost overnight and at a very young age whilst others develop in a much slower and unobtrusive way. Young girls can be very self-conscious about this so be very tactful if you are broaching this subject and wait until you have a private moment. There is often some concern about the lumps that appear in the breasts at this time. Reassure your child that this is just a part of their breasts 'budding' and it is perfectly normal. These small lumps will disappear eventually. You should also tell them that it is normal for the breasts to be quite tender and itchy at this time. To encourage a positive attitude to these developments you could suggest that you go on a shopping trip together to celebrate their developing figure and buy them some pretty new underwear. Make a day out of it, maybe going for lunch or doing something else that your daughter would like. All of this helps build up self-esteem. Equally, if your daughter seems anxious because she isn't developing at the same rate as her friends just reassure her that she will most certainly develop in her own time. If you were a late developer tell her about this and even if you weren't maybe a little white lie might make her feel better.

Some girls can be quite resistant to wearing a bra. If this is the case with your daughter listen to her reasons before dismissing them and try to come to some compromise such as a cami top which is softer and easier to wear than a bra whilst still giving a little support.

Pubic Hair

Some girls dread getting pubic hair and others can't wait. Most develop pubic hair before they get their first period, but not always. There are no set rules. I am often asked by children 'why do we get pubic hair?' There are a number of reasons but it is generally accepted that the main reason is that it surrounds an opening in our body and, as with our nostrils, the hair is there to stop irritants entering the body and for protection as the area surrounding the vagina is very sensitive. Pubic hair is a different texture to the hair on our head and usually a shade or two darker. I am occasionally asked by eleven-/twelve-year-old girls if they 'should' remove this hair, usually by waxing. I would always encourage them to leave well enough alone as it is a perfectly normal development and there is no logical reason for removing it.

Underarm and Leg Hair

The hair under the arms is often one of the last stages of development. As with pubic hair this varies greatly, with some girls growing quite thick hair in their armpits and others only ever getting a few strands. Most girls at some point choose to remove this hair; this is a personal choice. If your daughter wants to remove this hair talk to her about safe and effective ways of doing so. Shaving can be a bit hazardous in the beginning. There were occasions when the bathroom at home looked like the scene of the chainsaw massacre when I first started shaving. You may not want her to remove body hair at this point, or indeed ever, but if she does you should listen to her reasons for wanting to before dismissing the idea out of hand. If you agree that she may remove underarm or leg hair discuss the options, e.g. waxing (in a salon), depilatory cream, laser or shaving (I would suggest an electric shaver as there is less chance of severing an artery).

There is an old wives' tale that shaving makes the hair grow faster and thicker but believe it or not this is totally untrue. The regrowth of the hair will, however, have a blunt edge rather than a tapered one, which can make it feel courser. It is best not to shave the hair around the bikini area as this can cause ingrown hairs which can sometimes cause spots and be quite painful.

Heavier Perspiration

During puberty both boys and girls start to perspire more and the perspiration develops a stronger odour. This is due to the increase in hormone production and it was the way in which our distant ancestors attracted a mate. I somehow don't think a smell of sweat would do the same for this generation. Encourage your adolescents to shower every day if possible and use deodorant on clean skin and not to mask the smell of perspiration. Roll-ons are better for the environment and a bit safer for them to use as they can get aerosol burns if the canister is held too close to the skin. It is true that some people perspire more than others and the food we eat can affect the smell of our perspiration, for instance if you eat a lot of garlic or spicy food the smell can continue to be secreted through the pores for a few days after consumption in some instances.

Oily/Spotty Skin

During puberty the skin produces more sebum (an oily substance secreted by the sebaceous glands) and in some people this can lead to blocked pores and spots. Children and teenagers often label even very minor outbreaks on the face as acne, which of course it isn't. Acne is a very specific condition which requires medical intervention but can be successfully treated. It is very common for adolescents to have a few spots from time to time, so they should be encouraged to wash their face properly, morning and night, drink plenty of water, eat lots of fruit and vegetables, and get plenty of sleep (good luck with that). There are many medicated face washes on the market that can be very effective in helping to improve the appearance of skin breakouts.

Contrary to popular belief, fried food and chocolate do not give you spots but if your children don't have a balanced diet their skin, along with other organs, can be affected. Girls often find their skin is more prone to spots the week leading up to their period and their hair is often noticeably oilier at this time also. The use of a toner for their skin when this happens might help but I would suggest that they don't use a toner every day and to look for the mildest one available specifically for teenage skin. If they are going to squeeze blackheads tell them to wash their hands first and clean the area surrounding the blackhead. You can buy blackhead poppers in chemists. Be warned though this can trigger a lifetime obsession with popping. Take it from one who knows.

Widening of the Hips

Hormone production during puberty causes the hips to widen and the bottom to become rounder. This is because the pelvic area of women needs to be wider than that of men to facilitate pregnancy and childbirth. Some girls refer to this as 'getting their figure' and are quite proud of it whilst others really hate it. Up to this girls' and boys' body shape have been practically the same. Once again be really careful about referring to this with your daughter as they may be self-conscious. Another very common body development at this time is that they may also put on weight on their legs and thighs. All of these changes will be more noticeable with some girls than others.

More girls than boys seem to fall prey to the pressure to be slim or have particular attributes that may be fashionable at the time (usually propagated by celebrities). For some girls this can create unrealistic expectations and in more vulnerable girls it can even contribute to body dysmorphia and eating disorders. Some young and not-so-young girls think that they can change their natural body shape by diet or exercise, which is not the case. Body shape is a different issue to weight and can only be modified very slightly by diet and exercise. However, having a healthy body weight will give somebody confidence and therefore make them feel more attractive than being over- or underweight so encourage your daughter to embrace her shape, eat healthily and exercise as much as possible. Then throw away the bathroom scales!

Growth

Most girls have reached their full height by the time they are about fifteen years old; some however will continue to grow for another few years. They generally do not have such obvious growth spurts as boys but some girls can have a very obvious growth spurt around the time their first period makes an appearance and this will last varying amounts of time. The main contributory factors involved in height are genetics and hormones. Usually if a child has tall parents they will also be tall and vice versa but this is not always the case as there could be tall or small genes in previous generations. So it is not that unusual to have a small child in a tall family or a tall child in a small family.

Menstruation (Periods)

So what is this exactly? Every month after the onset of puberty a woman releases an egg from her ovary and creates a lining in her uterus in which the egg implants should it be fertilised by a sperm. If the egg is not fertilised the lining of the uterus will break away and be shed from the vagina. This is commonly referred to as a period.

Below I address some of the most common questions I am asked by girls regarding their first period.

'What Signs Might I Have Before I Get My Period?'

Well for some girls there are no signs at all until they see the stain in their pants. For others, they may have had cramps in their tummies, increased sensitivity in their breasts, swollen, hard tummies, increased vaginal discharge (a bit darker in colour than usual) or back ache. Their first period is viewed with a mixture of excitement and terror. What they need is reassurance that their period is a good sign and that their bodies are behaving exactly as they are designed to behave. Explain that the reason the discharge can sometimes appear to be brownish in colour before a period is because it can be mixed with blood. The first period can last as short as one day or as long as a week. At first periods are often irregular; girls may get a period that lasts a few days and then disappears for a few months or they get more than one bleed in a month. Some have perfectly regular cycles right from the beginning but these are the exception rather than the rule. The most common pattern for periods is to bleed for between three and seven days and have twenty-one to twenty-three days between each period. Encourage your daughter to make a note, either on a calendar or in her diary, each time she gets a period and she should eventually see a pattern forming, or for those who prefer there are a number of free apps that can be downloaded for logging periods, symptoms, etc. on your phone. If after a year she is still experiencing very irregular periods it might be useful to have a chat with your family doctor.

'Will They Be Really Painful?'

The answer to this is 'they shouldn't be'; some people experience more discomfort than others and some none at all. If your daughter's periods are excessively heavy or painful don't let her suffer on. There are various options open to her but the first step is to talk to your family doctor. As a young teenager I had heavy, irregular and painful periods but out of embarrassment I didn't tell anyone. Eventually at fifteen I went to my GP who referred me to a gynaecologist and eventually the problem was dealt with. It is worth checking in with your daughter every now and then to establish that her periods are not too uncomfortable whilst not making her feel like an invalid. A certain amount of discomfort is to be expected, rolling around in pain is not. Over-the-counter pain relief, a hot water bottle on the tummy or the back and a bit of TLC is usually all that is needed.

'What Pads Should I Use and How Do I Use Them?'

There are any number of pads to choose from. Thank God the big 'mouse hammocks' that my generation were subjected to are a thing of the past. Start with the smaller regular pads and if needs be your daughter can move on to the larger pads for a heavier flow. Be explicit about the changing of pads; the number of girls who believe you just have to put on a pad in the morning and leave it there for the day is quite astonishing. A pad usually needs changing about four times per day – morning, midday, evening and bedtime – unless they have a very slight flow in general or it is one of their light days, in which case they could get away with twice a day. If they have a heavy bleed explain that the pad may need to be changed more often and they should check regularly to avoid any leaks. Some people bleed quite heavily at nighttime so be prepared and buy her some nighttime pads; these are larger and more absorbent. Always explain what she should do with the used pads because they can get very embarrassed about disposing of them and sometimes try to flush them down the toilet. Show your daughter how to wrap the used pad in the plastic wrapping from the clean pad and tell her to dispose of it in the general waste bin. In school and public toilets there are designated bins for the disposal of used pads. Alternatively, it can be put inside a small bag (nappy bag) and disposed of in the general waste bin.

Eleven- and twelve-year-old girls are often very worried about getting their first period in school which might result in them having to ask their teacher for a pad, especially if their teacher is a man. You could reassure them that their teacher will be understanding but if they do not want to explain that they are having a period to a male teacher they should just ask to go to the office and speak to the secretary who will usually have pads for this very purpose. You could of course buy her some pads so she can keep one in her school bag or uniform pocket in case it is needed, which would probably be more reassuring for her. Girls in general seem much happier with this suggestion than asking their teacher for one. If your daughter has her periods and her teacher is male it might be a good idea for you to have a private word to explain that she has started menstruating and if she should ask to go to the toilet outside of the normal time not to question the reason for this. Another suggestion for dealing with periods in school is a 'take and replace' system. A pack of pads is left in the girls' toilet and if somebody needs one they can take one and bring a replacement in the next day.

'What about Tampons? How Old Do You Have to Be? Are They Dangerous?'

I would not really recommend tampons for the average eleven-/twelve-year-old because they can be a bit tricky to use at first and can be quite uncomfortable if not inserted properly. If you and your daughter decide that she should use tampons as opposed to pads or as well as pads I would suggest you use the type with an applicator. Some manufacturers make tampons that are especially designed for girls who have recently started menstruating so look out for 'teen tampons'. Read the instruction leaflet together so that you can answer any questions she might have. A tampon should be changed every few hours at least and never left in place for more than eight hours and absolutely never be used overnight. She should always ensure that the last tampon of a period is removed from the vagina as this is the most likely one to be forgotten about and a condition called Toxic Shock Syndrome can occur if this happens. Having said this, if used properly and with care they are very useful, particularly if she wants to go swimming or go to the beach and wear a swimsuit or bikini when she is having a period. Used tampons should be disposed of in the same way as pads in the general waste bin.

'Sometimes I Get Lumpy Bits in My Period – Is This Dangerous?'

These lumpy bits are clots and are quite normal. A period is not really blood as we know it; it is the lining of the uterus being shed because the egg that was released during ovulation wasn't fertilised so therefore the lining that built up in the uterus at this time isn't needed. As it is being shed sometimes bits of this lining can be released as a clot. Occasionally one of these clots can be quite large and can even be felt slipping out through the vagina; when this happens it can soak a pad immediately so explain that if she notices this sensation she should change her pad as quickly as possible.

Myths around Menstruation

Some of the old myths persist, such as you shouldn't have a bath or wash your hair when you have a period. These myths are not so widely held as they were when I was a teenager but I still get asked all too frequently why you shouldn't have a bath when you're having a period. I really don't know where or why that myth started but we should encourage more baths or showers when girls are menstruating, not less, and they may find that their hair needs washing even more often at this time because it can be quite oily just before and during a period. Whilst being sympathetic if our daughters are feeling a bit under the weather during menstruation is fine, we should not encourage them to think of themselves as sick and automatically need to take to the bed for the duration of their period. They will have a period once a month for approximately 40 years of their lives so that's an awfully long time spent in bed. Nor should periods be referred to as 'the curse' or 'our friends'. I've even heard them being referred to as a 'visiting aunt'. All of this feeds into the belief that there is something not nice or unclean about menstruation and the sooner we can move beyond this belief and accept menstruation as a normal part of a woman's life the better.

BOYS' DEVELOPMENT

A lot of the body developments in boys are similar to those in girls, such as increased perspiration, spots and body hair. So let's have a look at some of the differences.

Boys usually but not always start to develop physically a little later than girls, generally between the ages of eleven and thirteen. The hormone involved in this physical development is testosterone, produced in the testicles, which are glands contained in the scrotum, which is the sack that hangs behind the penis.

Facial Hair

This appears most usually around the age of thirteen or fourteen. It starts with a soft down and gradually thickens, particularly noticeable on the upper lip. Some boys sport this with pride while others can be quite embarrassed about it. There are no hard and fast rules as to when your son should start to shave; I would say as soon as he feels it is necessary. If possible, an older brother or dad could give them a few tips. But don't worry if this isn't possible; my son managed perfectly well without any input from his dad, as did my husband at that age. Boys' skin can be quite sensitive when they start shaving so it might help to buy an aftershave balm for them; there are lots of them on the market. Most boys are approximately fifteen years old when they first start shaving but some could be as young as twelve or thirteen.

Underarm and Leg Hair

This usually makes an appearance a little before facial hair starts to grow and unlike their sisters there is less pressure on them to remove it. Although it is becoming quite fashionable to do so now.

Pubic Hair

In my experience boys are delighted when they find their first pubic hair. It is a definitive sign that they are growing into young men. The pubic hair grows around the base of the penis on the lower abdomen and toward the back passage. It also usually grows in a triangle towards the naval and as with girls can often be a shade or two darker than head hair.

Chest Hair

The growth of chest hair varies greatly. Some men have absolutely no chest hair whilst others have a complete rug. Nearly all boys will develop some hair around the nipple area and are usually quite proud when they first become aware of this.

Broadening of the Shoulders

Boys' shoulders broaden and their pectoral muscles become more prominent during puberty; this is caused by the increased level of testosterone in their bodies. This will vary greatly depending on various factors such as the weight and physical build of the boy; however all boys will notice this to some extent. It is also perfectly normal for boys to notice little hard and sometimes painful lumps behind the nipple at this time. This does not mean that they are sprouting breasts and the lumps normally disappear within about a year.

Increased Sweat Production

As with girls more sweat is produced and the odour changes into a more adult odour so adolescent boys should be encouraged to shower more and start using a deodorant. It is also important to encourage them to change their socks and underwear on a daily basis as some boys can be a little reluctant to pay too much attention to their grooming at this age. It is not unusual for parents to have to beg, bribe or threaten their sons into the shower until they get to about fifteen years old - and then they can't get them out of it!

Spots

Most teenagers get a few spots, some more than others. As with girls, boys are also inclined to label even one spot 'acne'. They should be reassured that it is normal to get the occasional spot because of the increased production of an oily fluid called sebum. As with girls, reassurance and medical intervention when necessary is the key.

Development of the Penis and Testicles

The genitals start to become larger and slightly darker in colour as young as eleven in some boys and as old as sixteen in others. The average size of a fully grown penis in its soft/flaccid state is between five to seven centimetres and in its erect state approximately thirteen to fifteen centimetres. Even when a penis is less than five centimetres when flaccid the size when erect normally falls within the average range. Contrary to popular belief, height and shoe size are not an accurate indication as to the size of the penis. It is a good idea to encourage boys to gently retract the foreskin whilst in the bath or shower and make sure to wash and subsequently dry the head of the penis to prevent infection. It is not unusual for boys to have some problems with their foreskin, usually because it is too tight to retract, so remind them if they get any itching or soreness around the tip of the penis to tell you about it so you can get it checked out. Occasionally a circumcision is need but sometimes it is enough to gently massage the foreskin back on a regular basis until it becomes looser.

Sperm Production

Boys usually start to produce sperm anywhere between eleven and sixteen years of age, but most commonly between the ages of twelve and fourteen. The sperm is produced in the front of the testicles and stored in the back in the epididymis. Once a boy has started to produce sperm he will continue to do so for the rest of his life. Sperm live at one degree below body temperature and this is why the scrotum and testicles react to heat and cold, i.e. when the boy's body heats up the scrotum becomes looser to allow the testicles to get as far away from the body as possible to cool down and on a cold day or if the boy goes swimming in cold water the scrotum becomes tighter to bring the testicles up near the body to keep warm. Boys will produce millions of new sperm cells every day and the health and amount of sperm can be influenced by lifestyle factors, certain illnesses or in some cases genetics.

Wet Dreams

Once boys have started to produce sperm it is possible for them to have a 'wet dream'. It is called a wet dream because it happens during sleep. The sperm travel from the sperm store up the vas deferens, mix with semen, and travel down the urethra and out of the penis. In all there is about a teaspoonful of liquid released in this ejaculation, which is white and creamy in texture. Wet dreams do not necessarily mean that the boy has had a sexual or erotic dream; it can purely be the body's response to a full sperm store, although sometimes it is in response to a sexual or otherwise exciting dream. The average boy can expect to have between three and six wet dreams in a year, which usually decrease in frequency as they get older, although it is still possible that they will occur occasionally during adulthood. Many boys are told horror stories by older brothers or friends about this and can dread it happening, expecting to find themselves floating in a pool of liquid when they wake. It might be a good idea to reassure your son that it is perfectly normal and that if it happens they can just change their sheet if need be and there won't be any questions asked. For some reason many boys seem to think that mothers are forensic scientists who examine their sheets with blue lights when removing them for the wash.

Erections

Boys can experience erections at any age, even as new babies. An erection is the result of an extra supply of blood being diverted to the penis. Some erections are 'spontaneous', which means that they are not generated by sexual thoughts. These can happen at any time and can often be a source of embarrassment for boys. They can also be as a result of excitement other than sexual stimuli. Boys can experience erections due to sexual stimuli long before they have started producing sperm. This can be when they see something as simple as people kissing on television, reading something they find sexually interesting, or even just thinking about somebody they are attracted to.

Masturbation

This is a particularly tricky subject because of the private nature of the act. Most boys will not have any desire to talk about this with their parents or probably anybody else. In my experience of working with boys from the age of eleven up to eighteen years old it is quite normal for them to masturbate, some more than others. It can be an occasional act or in some cases a lot more than occasional; this varies from boy to boy, with age group and other external factors being an influence. First of all you should realise that it is perfectly normal and not something that needs to be 'dealt with'. From a very early age boys get some comfort from holding onto their penis; sometimes they don't even realise that they are doing it. It can be when watching television, going asleep or various other occasions. At some stage, probably during puberty, they will realise that it feels quite nice to massage their penis and once they have started producing sperm this will lead to ejaculation. Once this is done in private and doesn't become obsessive it is perfectly healthy and normal. If a boy does masturbate obsessively (a number of times each day), this can possibly be an indication that he has something on his mind and he's using masturbation to distract himself, or in some cases it can indicate that there is an excessive interest in pornography. Other than this there is absolutely nothing to worry about.

I realise that I have not referred to girls masturbating – which of course they do. Usually not as much as boys and not from such a young age but girls can also self-soothe in this way and again this is perfectly normal. We do of course have to address this if the child is constantly touching their privates in public but we should never make them feel that it is wrong or dirty. We can, however, remind them that this is a private part of their body and just as they would not go to the toilet in front of people they shouldn't do this in front of people either.

PART II

Older Teenagers: A Fly-On-The-Wall View

Topics of
Interest

12

A part of my work as a facilitator in the area of RSE was working with teenagers from fourteen to eighteen years of age, and over this next part of the book I am going to give you an insight into their attitudes, beliefs and concerns about their journey from adolescence to adulthood, where they come from, and the difficulties they sometimes have communicating them. Parents and teachers alike are often incredulous that teenagers would be prepared to open up about their lives and a lot of parents said to me that they would love to be a fly on the wall during one of my workshops. So that is precisely what I am going to do here – I am going to give you as close to a fly-on-the-wall view as I can.

One of the main misconceptions that adults in general have about teenagers is that if you ask them what aspect of relationships and sexuality they would like to talk about they are probably going to choose sex. I am not suggesting that they don't want to talk about sex but it was generally not considered by the teenagers I worked with to be the most important or interesting aspect of relationships. Maybe this was because I am quite matter-of-fact about this area and always explained to them in advance that they may choose any subject related to RSE that they would find useful to discuss – and that may include all types and aspects of relationships, sexuality and gender issues, conflict management, communication, expectations of relationships, sex and any other topics that would be useful to them to have discussed. They would make their suggestions anonymously in writing as this would give them absolute freedom of choice without any influence from classmates or members of the teaching staff if they were present.

The following is a list of topics that were routinely requested by most groups:

- Expectations of relationships
- Abusive relationships
- LGBT+ issues
- Sex (oral sex, anal sex, safe sex, consent)
  ◦ Pornography – effects on relationships
- Intimacy
- Mental health issues
- The effect of drink and drugs on relationships
- Unplanned pregnancies
- Toxic friendships
- How to deal with conflict in relationships
  ◦ Dealing with break-ups
  ◦ Family relationships

During the course of the following chapters I hope to give you some insight into the students' opinions, worries, hopes and expectations in connection with the above list. There will be a separate chapter for most of the topics but some (pornography, dealing with break-ups and family relationships) will be included in other chapters.

Expectations of Relationships

13

his topic always created interest in the groups because as teenagers they are still in the process of figuring out what are normal expectations for a relationship, what the opposite gender are looking for and indeed what others of the same gender are looking for. As a facilitator my job was to create an environment that encouraged people to share their opinions and not impose my opinions on them. I found it both interesting and enlightening to compare the expectations of boys and girls separately when at all possible (only possible in co-educational schools). To do this the boys would be asked to discuss their expectations and their understanding of girls' expectations and vice versa for the girls.

This exercise was always entered into with great enthusiasm and without exception the students found it interesting. Obviously some were more self-conscious than others and some a lot more experienced in this area than others, but even the less experienced members of the group still had expectations. The following is a list of the most commonly acknowledged expectations that students identified.

Boys think girls are looking for:

- Love
- Loyalty

- Trust
- Commitment
- Someone to talk to
- Protection
- Someone to make them laugh
- Romance
- Compliments
- Money
- Good body
- Someone who smells nice
- Someone who gets on with their friends
- Good teeth
- Good looks
- Big penis
- Sex

Girls say they are looking for:

- Someone to make them laugh
- Someone to protect them
- Loyalty
- Trust
- Physical attraction
- Someone who smells nice
- Someone who doesn't change when their friends are around
- A good listener
- A good kisser
- Sex (eventually)
- Someone to feel comfortable with

Girls think boys are looking for:

- Sex
- Blow jobs
- Good bodies – slim, big boobs and nice bum
- Someone who isn't clingy
- Good-looking

- Someone to talk to
- Someone to have a laugh with
- Trust
- Someone who gets on with their friends
- Sandwiches (what they probably mean is 'someone who is willing to make them a sandwich')

Boys say they are looking for:

- Loyalty
- Trust
- Fun
- Someone who gets on with their friends
- Netflix and chill!
- A good body
- Someone who isn't bitchy
- Hugs
- Food
- A good-looking girl
- Someone to talk to
- Nice teeth
- A girl who doesn't use too much makeup

As you can see, the boys' understanding of girls' expectations is a bit more comprehensive than the girls' understanding of boys' expectations. This is fairly representative of most groups irrespective of other background influences. This may be due to the fact that some girls find it easier than boys to talk about their needs and expectations, therefore giving boys a better insight. It may also be connected to the possibility of some boys wearing their emotional 'suit of armour'. As I mentioned earlier, many boys do not want to appear weak or needy and may have difficulty in being honest about their needs in a relationship, which in turn may impact on the way girls view boys.

A couple of years ago, whilst working on the area of expectations with a group of fifth-year students in a co-educational school, it became obvious that one boy in particular had the reputation of being a bit of 'ladies' man'. He was very affable and cooperative and quickly agreed to being the spokesperson for his particular discussion group. He proceeded to read out to the class the list of expectations from the group he was working with. Their list included affection, trust, loyalty, attraction, cuddles and sex, amongst other things. One of the girls seemed more than a little shocked that these expectations had come from the group that he was working with and said 'I bet you didn't choose any of those.' He said he had chosen most of them. She was more than a little sceptical about this, but the group he was working with confirmed that he was actually telling the truth. She was still more than a little reluctant to believe him and he said 'you probably think I just want sex. Everybody thinks that but it's just the way I talk.' I was pleasantly surprised at his candour and congratulated him. I asked the other boys in the class if they could identify with this and the vast majority of them said they could. The girls in the group were quite shocked because this kind of honesty in a public forum is very rare.

I think boys often shoot themselves in the foot by trying to hide their vulnerability and it becomes a self-fulfilling prophecy that instead of the intimacy and care that they really want they find themselves living up to the false image that has been created, not only by them but by generations of boys before them. This creates a kind of double jeopardy because even though some girls may be more than happy with less sexual contact, because of the general and often mistaken expectation that boys are mainly interested in a physical relationship they can sometimes interpret the boy not looking for sex as them not being attracted to them and occasionally it is the girls who push the sexual agenda, which for some boys can create more than a little pressure if they are not ready for this step.

By the time we reach adulthood it has become apparent to most of us that both genders have roughly the same requirements from relationships, but teenagers have not had the life experience to understand this. Expectations are fundamental to all relationships and understanding where these expectations come from and the ability to recognise which ones are negotiable provides one of the building blocks on which a committed relationship is built.

So where do we get our expectations from? Well the answer to this is very varied. We are influenced by our upbringing, friends, media, religion, society, etc. From the time we are born we are observing other people's relationships, even children raised by professional carers are still observing other people's relationships. Before we ever embark on a relationship we already have a script for that relationship implanted in our minds.

For example, I always expected that I would get married and have children; I expected that my husband would be the main breadwinner, that we would argue, that I would be the parent in charge of discipline, that my husband would play the role of the good cop (comic relief) in relation to the children, that our house would be a social place and in general I would be in charge. Unfortunately, my husband had his own script which was similar to mine in lots of ways but dissimilar in others - mostly not causing serious arguments other than on one or two points which were sources of major disagreement. Especially my expecting to be the one in charge! It was only after numerous arguments about parenting styles and how we dealt with conflict that I had a long, cold look at my expectations and why I had them. I couldn't believe the extent of the influence of my family of origin. As in most families of that period, my mother ran the house with little or no consultation with my father; she was the one we had to get permission from to do things and the one who made all important decisions as far as the children were concerned. This gave my dad the enviable position of just being the 'doting father and comic relief'; it is no wonder that he was far more popular with his daughters than my mother was! If you had asked me at the time would I use similar parenting techniques as my mother I would have emphatically said 'no', but despite this and without being aware I found myself adopting quite a lot of her parenting style. This being said, I was equally influenced by my father and decided that although I wanted to be the parent in charge of discipline I was going to be a lot more relaxed about it than my mother had been, and I didn't like it at all when my husband actively involved himself in the discipline of the children by telling them off if they were cheeky or imposing restrictions when he thought they needed them. This, after all, was my job! Did he not know his job was to be the comic relief? I would like to say that we sorted this out and we agreed as mature adults that there should be equal input from both parents but some things run far too deep and I never got used to him being firm with them, even though my more logical self knew this was not only his perfect right but a very good idea.

One of the most useful things I learned during my training as a facilitator was that 'if we don't understand our family we are in danger of repeating their mistakes.' This doesn't mean that you should blame your family for any perceived shortcomings – there is no such thing as the perfect family – but I found it helpful to try to understand why certain people in my family of origin behaved in certain ways and draw comparisons to some of my deeply held beliefs. So beware! You are being watched by your children and they will grow up either trying to emulate what they see or doing their best to avoid any similarity. Either way, the influence is equally there.

Our friends in turn are influenced by their families and they bring their own influences into play in our lives; teenagers generally don't like to be too out of step with their friends' attitudes so may find themselves adopting some values and expectations from their friends' families. We are all influenced by media but none more so than the young; songs, films, soaps, reality television and advertisements all have a subliminal influence on expectations. Think back to the way you were influenced by all of these things in your teens. Our attitudes to romance are often embedded in the music we listen to and the films we watch as young people. I was a child of the 60s and the message was to rebel, to be free, to be different. One of my favourite musicians was Bob Dylan, who espoused free love, anti-war and anti-establishment sentiments, which is one of the reasons I was attracted to my husband. He was a hippy who had lived in communes and hitched his way around

France and Spain: all of these things I found really attractive. My parents took an instant dislike to him for the same reason that I took an instant interest in him. I am pleased to say that he proved them wrong and they grew to love him when they realised that I wasn't going to run off to live in a commune.

Religious influence is not nearly as strong these days as it was fifty years ago. However, religion still has a part to play in the lives of some young people. Often they have come from homes where there is strong religious belief, while some teens can come from homes where religion plays no part at all but they have developed their own interest in it and this will have some influence on the choices they make going forward – which in itself is neither positive nor negative as long as they respect the right of others to either have a different religious affiliation or no interest in religion at all.

Even superficial expectations like who we find attractive can be influenced by all of the above, but especially by the media. This has been the case since there was a media. Trends in beauty, desirability, and so on change. For me it varied from Bob Dylan to Paul McCartney depending really on who my friends liked at the time; for my children it was Robbie Williams or Damon Albarn from Blur. We were just relieved when my oldest daughter stopped liking Kurt Cobain and we were no longer subjected to listening to his depressing dirge on any car journey that involved my daughter (one of which was from one end of Italy to the other!). All of this is fairly harmless and as we grow older and hopefully wiser we realise that who the person is rather than what they look like is what is important. Try telling that to a teenager though!

If you want to have a conversation with your teen about their expectations of relationships it might be a good idea to firstly familiarise yourself with your own, and if you have a partner compare them with theirs. Don't worry if you find that your expectations and those of your partner are not completely compatible; we are not meant to be clones of each other. It could lead to an interesting conversation though. I would also add at this point that expectations change throughout life but needs do not. Needs are basic and non-negotiable. Expectations are desires or wishes and are negotiable.

The following are needs; you may have more but these are some basic ones:

- Safety
- Honesty
- Respect
- Equality

Expectations are far more varied but are likely to include some of the following:

- Love
- Romance
- Fidelity
- Warmth
- Sex
- Attraction
- Fun
- Children
- Intimacy
- Holidays

Your children may never have thought about needs and expectations of a relationship before but if they can identify these at this stage they will be in a far better position to ensure that their needs are met and at least some of their expectations are realised.

A good way to start a conversation with your teen would be to say 'Have you got a type?' They may 'yes' or 'no, not really'; either way you can open up the conversation by telling them what your type was at their age, if it has changed, why you think you were attracted to a particular type, etc. If they are happy with the conversation you can enlarge on it to include how important or unimportant they think the following topics are with regard to relationships:

- *Background* - would they think that it is important that the person they were attracted to has a similar family background? They will probably say 'no'; however, research shows that people coming from similar backgrounds have a better chance of a successful relationship as they have a greater understanding of one another's values.
- *Religion* - you will probably already have a good idea as what they will say about this. Remember the aim is not to change their opinion, just to hear what it is. Of course a healthy exchange of views might ensue, which is fine as long as you don't feel the need for consensus or agreement.
- *Attitude to children* - would they like children? What kind of mother or father do they think they would be? What kind of mother or father would they like their partner to be? If they would like children but met somebody they loved who didn't want children would this impact on their decision to be with that person? How do they see the management of children and work being organised - who would be the parent most likely to sacrifice a career if necessary to care for children?
- *Money* - how important is it to them? As parents you will have a good insight already about their attitude to this. Can you have a good relationship if there is a shortage of money? Who do they see as the main breadwinner?
- *Attitude to drink and socialising* - would they see their future home being a social place? Would it be important for their partner to have a similar attitude? How important is it to maintain friendships after marriage or entering into a long-term relationship?

I would try to be as casual as possible whilst doing this; don't get the pen and paper out. Make it conversational and don't use it as an opportunity to change their opinions. Remember this is about getting to know what they think at this time, no more, no less.

Abusive Relationships

14

The vast majority of students I have worked with request the inclusion of a discussion on abusive or dysfunctional relationships. I am not sure if they are just more aware of this problem or if the problem is becoming more widespread amongst their age group. This, as you will appreciate, needs to be handled with tact and diplomacy as it is so important not to leave anybody feeling vulnerable or 'outed'. The most useful approach was to discuss the subject generally and ask for their input. One of the ways to do this was by requesting them to work in small groups to discuss how they see the lifeline of abuse unfolding in teenage relationships. The following is a summary from a large number of groups. The list is from minor, fairly common situations to more harmful and downright dangerous ones:

- Wanting to spend too much time together
- Always asking who is texting/messaging you
- Wanting to check your phone
- Checking your social media accounts and grilling you about the content
- Being jealous of time spent with friends and family
- Criticising appearance - saying things like 'I am just telling you for your own good', etc.

- Demanding that you only spend time with them
- Threatening you, either with violence or with leaving you
- Pushing, shoving, hitting and other methods of violence, such as sexual violence

Not all abusive relationships are physically abusive; some use manipulation or language that over a period of time damages or destroys the victim's self-esteem. Most physical abusers are male but that is not to say that women never physically abuse men or indeed another woman. It is less common, however, for a male to report being a victim of either physical or other forms of abuse. This again is possibly connected to the suit of armour that some men wear to prevent others seeing their vulnerability and shame, but is also due to the fact that women are less likely to physically abuse a man than the other way around. All abuse, whether it is emotional or physical, is about control and can be present in family relationships, friendships or romantic relationships. Giving teenagers the time and space to examine dispassionately how and why relationships become dysfunctional is essential as once they have become embroiled in a dysfunctional relationship it can be very hard for them to recognise it as such. Unfortunately, through my involvement in this area I have spoken to quite a few girls who after they have been given the opportunity to examine this topic have identified either themselves, a friend or a family member as being in an abusive relationship. I have spoken to fewer boys in this position but I have spoken to boys who feel they are being manipulated by their girlfriend/boyfriend into staying with them when they feel the relationship is over for them. This may not sound as problematic as physical abuse but I have spoken to some young people who have been really distressed because they do not know how to deal with this problem.

This must be one of the hardest conversations a parent ever has to have with their child and one that thankfully is still relatively uncommon. The key point for parents who find themselves in this situation is to listen to what your child is saying without being too eager to jump in with your avenging angel costume on. Even though this response would be perfectly normal, it may close the conversation down prematurely. Most people in abusive or dysfunctional relationships know they need help. They may not come right out and say they do but they often drop hints, hoping that the person they are talking to will either question them further or at least offer some advice. As parents we of course should be vigilant without jumping to half-baked conclusions. If your teenage child comes home with a cut or a bruise and says that they have fallen whilst they are out do not immediately assume that their boyfriend/girlfriend is abusive (even if you don't happen to like them. In fact, especially if you don't happen to like them) as by doing this you have immediately demonstrated that you either do not like or do not trust their boyfriend/girlfriend and this may create a problem with future conversations should your son/daughter want to talk to you. If, however, they are becoming withdrawn, losing contact with friends, changing their appearance, closing down social media accounts or you notice any other significant change in their usual personality it is worth sitting them down privately and outlining your concerns, or better still try to get them away somewhere nice with you for a few days if at all possible. You should explain to them that you are there to listen and offer whatever help they need. Reassure them that you are not going to make them do anything they are unhappy about; after all if there is a problem the last thing they need is another person telling them what to do.

The most important thing you can do to help your child if you think there is a problem is to keep the conversation flowing; do not allow yourself or other family members to be pushed out of their life and tell them if they don't feel comfortable talking to you they could talk to another adult they trust. If they do tell you that their girlfriend/boyfriend has become manipulative or abusive in any way you should tell them that they need to leave the relationship and if the abuse is serious they should inform the Gardaí and the parents of the person who is perpetrating the abuse, particularly in the case of physical abuse or other threatening behaviour. Thankfully the area of domestic abuse is taken far more seriously than in previous generations and is constantly under review. In 2018 legislation was enacted which covers coercive control, an aspect of abuse that previously was not legislated for in Ireland.

Below are some examples of abusive relationships that I have encountered in the course of my work, which may give you more insight into and a possible introduction to a tricky but very important subject.

The first example is that of an eighteen-year-old girl who reported being in an abusive relationship to the facilitator after a workshop. She had been in a relationship with her boyfriend for approximately one year. She said he was normally attentive and kind and she really liked him. However, he was becoming more controlling and didn't want her to spend time with her friends to the point that he would threaten to break up with her if she did. He was also very critical of said friends and their very normal teenage behaviour. He questioned her incessantly and monitored her phone and social media use. She put up with this because she really liked him and, as she said, he could be attentive, kind and charming. He was also very good-looking and popular and on one level he was a trophy boyfriend. The problem came to a head when she wanted to go out to celebrate a friend's eighteenth birthday; she knew it would be pointless suggesting this to her boyfriend so she told him that she was sick and was going to bed early. During the night out with her friends she received a number of texts suggesting that he should come around to her house and keep her company but she made the excuse that she really wasn't up to it and was just going to go asleep. At the end of the night she got a taxi home only to find him waiting outside her house. Needless to say he was very angry that he had been deceived and he became violent, head-butting her and breaking her nose. She went into the house and went to bed without telling anybody what had happened. During the course of the night she was bombarded with messages of apology and assurances that this would never happen again whilst at the same time blaming her for causing the problem in the first place. When she got up the next morning her parents were horrified at her injury but rather than telling them the truth she told them that she had fallen when she got out of the taxi. They brought her to the hospital and as far as they were concerned it was an unfortunate accident. Needless to say, this made her very nervous of upsetting him again but she still was not prepared to end the relationship. That was until she participated in the workshop exercise outlining the progression of abuse and she could see that her relationship fitted this model perfectly. It was what was needed to give her the strength and encouragement to do the right thing and get the help that she needed, which she did with the assistance of her parents. If she hadn't taken part in that workshop, however, the outcome could possibly have been very different.

The second case is maybe not as dramatic but nonetheless very upsetting for the person concerned. A seventeen-year-old boy told me that he was caught up in a relationship with a girl whom he didn't want to be with but every time he tried to break up with her she threatened to kill herself. He said that he knew when he went home from school she would be in his kitchen talking to his mum, who apparently loved her. I asked him had he told his mum what was happening and he said he had but she just told him that he would be mad to end the relationship and he would regret it. I am sure she did not intend to put the wishes of herself and the girl in question above her son's wishes but unfortunately that was exactly what was happening. The girl, according to the mum, was perfect for him and she told him that he was not to hurt her. His mother didn't want to accept that the girlfriend just wasn't what her son wanted. I told him he needed to put the responsibility for this girl back where it belonged and that was with her parents. He had a right to end the relationship as long as it was done respectfully, and he made it clear to the girl that he was going to speak to her parents about her state of mind. His mother was another matter - she would just have to learn to accept her son's judgement and not interfere in his love life.

The last example I will give you again involves a girl in a physically abusive relationship. This particular girl approached the facilitator after a workshop and said 'can you tell me how to stop being such a wreck-the-head?' She was asked what she meant by this and she said that she wrecked her boyfriend's head all of the time and she wanted to stop. When she was asked what she did to wreck his head she said, 'I never agree to anything; I moan all of the time and look for arguments.' Her friend who was present said 'tell her what he does to you', so she said 'he bites me.' When the facilitator asked her to elaborate she pulled up the sleeve of her shirt to display a number of bite marks down her arm, and she said that he also bit her on the inside of her thigh because he knew that hurt more. The facilitator in question was incredulous that this girl had put up with this behaviour for over a year. When she was asked why she was still in the relationship she said 'he only loses his temper with me because he loves me and he said if I stopped wrecking his head he'd never get angry with me.' This, of course, is a classic response of a victim taking on the responsibility for their abuser's behaviour. She was told that this behaviour is inexcusable and she would never stop wrecking his head because an abuser will always find a reason for their behaviour. The incident was reported to the school and the girl confirmed that she would inform both the Gardaí and her parents.

These incidents, I think you will agree, are really concerning and unfortunately are far from the only incidents of this kind that I have encountered during the course of my work. But what is even more concerning is that it is only the tip of the iceberg and for every teenager who speaks out there are probably ten others who suffer in silence. This may be because they don't want to lose their boyfriend/girlfriend or possibly because they have accepted the behaviour as normal, but whatever the reason we need to acknowledge the problem and empower young people to deal with it.

Hopefully by you talking about these incidents at home it might encourage more openness and could possibly even save a life. The conversation does not have to be a formal one. It could just be a case of 'do you know what I read in this book?' There are lots of other opportunities for raising the subject with your teenager, such as when abusive behaviour in portrayed or discussed on television programmes, news reports or newspaper articles. The main thing is that we talk about it and remove the veil of secrecy that is needed for this type of behaviour to thrive.

LGBTQ+
Teens

15

The school environment has definitely changed for the better in the last five years or so, with far greater acceptance of diversity - such as in the area of sexuality or gender. Students are generally encouraged to be inclusive and respectful in most schools and the gay or transgender student is less likely to feel excluded or alienated by the group. That is not to say that homophobia has been completely eradicated, as discussed in Chapter 9 regarding younger students, but it is less common than it once was and generally not tolerated by either the school or other students. That being said, even one case of bullying is one too many and it should be met with zero tolerance by all concerned.

Homophobic bullying has always been less common among female students but of late there has been a shift towards a more accepting and respectful attitude with the male student population also. So what has brought about this change for the better? I think one of the major changing points was the marriage equality referendum in 2015. This initiated some very useful discussions allowing people to talk openly about their worries, opinions and attitudes. I am not suggesting that all of the opinions expressed are purely positive or even positive at all, but this is normal and healthy. At least we are talking and therefore hopefully reaching a greater under-standing of what life is like for the LGBTQ+ student.

SEXUALITY

The discussions that I facilitated in secondary schools centred around relationships and what effect gender and sexuality has on this. Students were asked to discuss the needs and expec-tations of a couple in a gay relationship as opposed to those in a heterosexual relationship. Initially they often assume that the expectations of a gay couple are quite different to the expectations of a heterosexual couple. However, when asked to identify the differences they were hard-pushed to find any because of course they don't exist. There may be some slight nuances and variations, particular in the area of children and family, but the fundamental needs and expectations are the same. Occasionally students may cite sex as being one of the differences, but when asked to examine this further there is usually a general consensus that expectations around sex are different from couple to couple irrespective of gender or sexu-ality anyway. The physical aspect of sex does not have that many variations and it involves the same parts of the body just utilised in slightly different ways from couple to couple, irrespective of sexuality. What is far more important than this is how the couple communicate with each other on their needs, hopes, fears, dislikes, desires, etc. Can they be totally honest with each other without fear of rejection? Do they try their best to respect their partner's wishes and feelings? And do they accept the shared sexual experience as part of a loving, intimate relationship? If this is the case their chromosomes are of little or no importance.

I have spoken to a large number of parents over the years with many different views regarding sexuality and their children. Some parents are very open to the possibility of their child being gay, bisexual, asexual, etc., whilst others would view it as a major problem. Whatever your view you cannot change who your son or daughter is. There are some parents who think that by making their views explicit this will stop their child from developing what they see as a 'problem' – which of course is complete rubbish. What it will do is create a very unhappy child who may deny who they are even to themselves. I am happy to say that this is the exception rather than the rule though. I do realise that it can be a shock or a worry for some parents when they discover that their child is gay/bi. Even some loving and generally open-minded parents may worry about how their child will be accepted by family and society in general, or they mourn the loss of the possibility of becoming grandparents. Of course neither of these things should be a concern. Most people are more accepting of same-sex relationships so thankfully it is no longer something that should be perceived as a problem and those who cannot accept gay relationships as valid are the ones with the problem, not the people in the gay relationship. As far as grandchildren are concerned, being in a same-sex relationship does not preclude you from being parents.

How parents handle this situation will be different from family to family, with some having a purely positive reaction and others unfortunately not. I have spoken to parents from both camps and sometimes the extreme of both camps. Their reaction may be influenced by culture, age, family background, religion, media, etc. Obviously the parents who are completely positive and sometimes even overly enthusiastic are going to cause far fewer problems than the parent who is negative or hostile to the news.

You may ask how could a parent be overly enthusiastic so I will give you an example of a conversation I had with a sixteen-year-old girl. She approached me after a workshop and said 'I think I'm gay' to which I responded 'is this a problem?' She said that she still wasn't sure but felt that she was being pushed into pinning her colours to the mast, so to speak, by a couple of friends and her mum. She loved her mum and she said that she had been really positive when she told her that she thought she was gay but she didn't hear the word 'thought'. She really just wanted to put it out there and possibly talk about her feelings but her mum immediately took up the baton and started talking about girlfriends, wanting to tell family, etc. The girl had to quite firmly tell her mum to stop, saying 'I only said I thought I was gay; I didn't say I was definitely gay!' She was still growing used to the fact herself and, like most teenagers, didn't want to commit just in case she was wrong. As she said herself, what if she wasn't gay and she had told everyone she was? I told her that she should relax; it isn't like joining a club with a limited membership so if you miss the chance to join today you may never get in. I told her to just enjoy being who she was and allow herself to accept her feelings and accept that they are prone to change from day to day at this age, and most importantly not give in to the pressure, well-meaning or otherwise, to make any declarations. I didn't have any worries for this girl because she was surrounded by love and had a well-meaning if somewhat overly enthusiastic mother so whatever conclusion she came to she would probably be happy.

I have, however, unfortunately encountered the total opposite of this on more than one occasion. One particularly upsetting example of this happened in a community school with a group of fifth-year students. During the workshop I noticed that one particular student seemed quite withdrawn and not comfortable with joining in some of the discussions. This girl was of a different cultural background so I put it down to this. At the end of the workshop a boy approached me with this same girl in tow. He said 'she needs to talk to you' and when I looked at her she had tears running down her cheeks. I asked her what was wrong and she said that she was gay but she couldn't let her parents know as they would be really angry and throw her out of the house. I asked her how she knew this would be their reaction and she said they had told her. When I questioned her further about what inspired them to say this she said they suspected she was gay and a big argument took place which culminated in her denying it. I asked her what help she was getting and she said that she was really lucky to have the support of the boy who accompanied her who was also gay, and in turn had the support of his family who apparently were very loving toward her. She also found the backup of BelongTo invaluable. I asked her what her plan was and she said that as soon as she had done her Leaving Cert and secured a college place she would leave home and didn't want to see her parents again. I found this incredibly sad. Here were two parents who I am sure loved their child in their own way but had totally alienated her because she did not fit the image of who they expected her to be.

I cannot stress enough how we as parents need to deal with this subject with respect and sensitivity. Remember this is not a lifestyle choice or a fad and you won't, as some people think, 'turn somebody gay' by being too accepting; neither will you stop somebody from being gay by forbidding it.

My own son was 22 when he told me he was gay. I can honestly say that I was not expecting it; so much for 'gaydar'. However, I can also just as honestly say that my only concern was that he was happy, which he said he was. I told him that it made no difference to me whatsoever and that any future boyfriends would be very welcome in our home. My husband was in bed asleep at the time so when he woke up the next morning I told him the news, to which he responded 'I'd better go in and hug him before I set off for work.' If you are curious as to why my son waited so long to have the conversation with me it was simply that he didn't know for sure he was gay, which is perfectly normal and far from uncommon. For some people there is no doubt at all from a fairly young age but for others it is more of a gradual dawning, often not becoming really apparent until adulthood. He has since married and he and his husband are really happy; and we have another much-loved member of our family. I realise that my reaction is not necessarily yours but it might be worthwhile as parents to ask yourself what your response would be in this instance and if you have negative views or concerns try to understand where they are coming from and ask yourself what impact these may have on your child should they happen to be gay or bisexual. I think most parents just want to do the right thing by their children and, above all, we want them to be happy and to find someone to love who loves them in return, and it should not be important whether that person is the same or the opposite gender.

Transgender Issues

Whilst it is true that there are more students than ever questioning their gender or going through gender reorientation it is still a relatively rare and misunderstood phenomenon by both the young and not-so-young. Issues regarding gender have frequently become apparent before the person reaches their teens but not always. I gave an example in Chapter 9 of how one family dealt with the transitioning of their ten-year-old.

For the young person involved there are often emotional problems associated with gender issues, including depression, self-harm and eating disorders. This may be due to the fact they could be finding it really hard to express what they are feeling, especially if they have not addressed it earlier in their life, or it could even be that they themselves are resistant to what they are feeling. I can't imagine how hard this must be, especially if you think your family, particularly your parents, are going to be unaccepting. Statistics show that 78 per cent of trans people have suicidal ideation and 40 per cent of them have attempted suicide. What a startlingly awful statistic! Surely that only goes to prove how imperative it is that we have more open conversations regarding this issue in the media and more practical help for those parents and young people who need it. For those of us who don't need help in this area we should show empathy to those who do and do our best to educate ourselves and deal with the subject respectfully and with understanding, bearing in mind that it could be your child, grandchild or other family member in the future.

A part of the adjustment for parents of the trans child is a possible sense of mourning for the child they gave birth to whilst striving to accept the new identity of their son/daughter. Thankfully there are experienced counsellors available to help both the young person and their family; TENI (the Transgender Equality Network of Ireland) or BelongTo (the national organisation supporting LGBTI+ young people in Ireland) will be happy to recommend one in your area. In my experience, friends and most other students react positively but there are still those who may still struggle to understand so I think we should be encouraging our schools to ensure that information on gender equality is included in SPHE as this is the only way to both dispel myths and create an environment of respect and understanding.

Should you suspect your son or daughter may be having questions regarding their gender just listen to what they say. What you do not need to do is to assume that you need to do anything other than try to understand what they are telling you. Don't make judgements, don't overreact and most of all don't tell them they are wrong to be feeling what they are feeling. They may be quite confused and more than a little scared so what they need most is your support. Remember if there is an actual problem it will become apparent and if this is the case either of the above organisations have the expert help to guide you through it.

16

Sex

Of course most teenagers are curious about sex. I know I was as a teenager and I'm sure most of you were. It is new and exciting to them; they are newly fertile and Mother Nature is prodding them forward into sexual activity, and not very gently in some cases.

It is true that attitudes have changed since you were a teenager, but then attitudes were probably not the same then as in your parents' youth. One of the main changes is the amount of information available to young people and not all of it is necessarily useful or even completely wholesome, but a lot of teenagers are very capable of deciphering fact from fiction regarding this.

Your children's worries, hopes, etc. are probably not too different from yours at their age. Some teenagers will start experimenting with sexual activity from a fairly young age. For some this will just be kissing or intimate touching, but for others it could be oral sex or sexual intercourse. However, there are some who make a conscious decision to delay serious sexual activity until they are over seventeen or eighteen, or until they are in a serious long-term relationship such as marriage.

Some parents are open to their teenage sons and daughters being sexually active whilst others would be horrified at the prospect. Again the attitudes of parents are probably influenced by their upbringing, religious beliefs, society, media, etc. There is a fine line between wanting to protect our children and being totally unrealistic about the fact that they have sexual desires. If you do not talk openly and listen to your children, but rather lay down the law about what you expect from them, they may just become more secretive and develop more skilful ways of keeping you in the dark. That isn't to say that you are not entitled as parents to tell your children that you would prefer if they delayed sexual activity until they are older, but I think you need to talk reasonably to them about why you think this is a good idea, and before you talk to them it would help if you understand why you have reached this decision yourself. To do that you need to look back at the messages you received about sex when you were younger. Were they mainly positive or negative? Were they loaded with fear and warnings or were you not told anything at all? The last thing you want to do is make them think that sexual attraction or enjoyment of sex is wrong or dirty.

I believe most parents want their children, both boys and girls, to be treated with respect and to treat others in the same way. Most parents would also say that they want their children to be selective and only have sex when it is a part of a loving relationship whilst being realistic that this is not always the case. One message that I believe is important for teenagers to hear is that sex should be a positive experience, enjoyed by both parties; it should enhance the sense of closeness in a relationship; it should never make you doubt yourself; and of course it should at all times be safe. So if there is a need to seek reassurance after sex or there is an underlying sense of rejection or disrespect and their instinct is telling them that something is not right they should trust this instinct. It was probably either the wrong person or the wrong reason, or maybe both, and they should avoid having sex with that person again or at the very least not until a conversation has been had about their needs and expectations.

One commonly held myth is that boys are always more interested in sex than girls. Whilst some boys are very interested in sex I have spoken to a large number of boys over the years who have said that they just don't feel ready but feel they are being pressured into being sexually active, sometimes by friends and sometimes but less often by girls. They generally feel very relieved when told that it is perfectly normal to either not want or not feel ready for sex at their age. Because of the sensitivity of the subject I would usually suggest anonymous written feedback regarding possible concerns and the following list is representative of this feedback:

- Fear of 'being no good at it' - being laughed at or talked about - and the impact of pornography
- Penis size
- Safe sex
- Consent - what does this really mean and how do you know if someone has consented?
- Unplanned pregnancy

FEAR OF FAILURE OR 'NOT BEING GOOD AT IT', AND THE IMPACT OF PORNOGRAPHY

I would imagine these fears have been around for quite some time but are probably magnified now by the ready availability of pornography. Most teenage boys and a lot of teenage girls have viewed pornography to some extent. Part of this is due to the natural curiosity surrounding this subject but unfortunately there are some who develop a habit or even addiction in this area. When this topic comes up for discussion in the classroom and the question 'how many of your friends watch pornography regularly?' is asked, usually 95–97 per cent of boys' hands would be raised and maybe 10 per cent of girls'. This is not necessarily a totally accurate reflection but it is the most common answer that students give. So how do they feel pornography affects them and their relationships?

Pornography generally depicts sexual activity in a performance-related way or as an act perpetrated against one person for the enjoyment of the other. What it does not depict, to the best of my knowledge, is mutually respectful, caring love-making which involves a grown-up dialogue about what is about to take place. Even when the acts are highly unlikely to be enjoyable for one of the parties (usually the woman) she still may appear to be enthusiastically involved and making the mandatory sound effects. This may lead young men to form the opinion that they should be able to deliver the same performance in real life and indeed this is probably what girls in general expect of them, which may compound their fear that if they can't there is probably something wrong with them.

It is still the case that more young men than young women watch porn. Pornography is an industry that is predominantly driven by men for the enjoyment of men. If a person is over eighteen, which is the legal age for viewing pornographic material, it is entirely their choice if they wish to do so and I am sure there are many adults who occasionally watch pornography for enjoyment without any ill effects as their attitudes and expectations of sex are probably already formed. The worry is that children as young as ten years old can and do access pornography and some of them will become habitual viewers. It is inevitable that this will affect their expectations of themselves as sexual beings and their expectations of any future sexual partners. From discussions in the classroom on this topic I have found that the vast majority of young men realise that they are being peddled a myth but habitual viewing of porn and the subsequent discussions with friends who may also be hooked into the same behaviour can desensitise them and the line between fiction and reality can become blurred. It can also endorse the attitude that sexual gratification is more important than building up an intimate relationship because, as they may see it, the actresses in these films do not require intimacy and they would seem to be very comfortable with being used in a sexual way so this could possibly lead to the belief that all girls should be equally comfortable with this. The extreme of this of course is sexual assault. Whilst the majority of boys that I speak to would be appalled at the idea of forcing a girl to have sex, there has been some evidence to suggest that the constant viewing of pornography can fudge boundaries for some people.

As well as unrealistic expectations surrounding sexual activity, pornography also influences expectations of body image, particularly amongst young people who are still in the process of reaching sexual and physical maturity. The widely held belief that any body hair on a woman is unacceptable and that breasts should be perfectly shaped and a minimum of a D cup, or that boys should have at least a six-pack if not an eight-pack and should be groomed to within an inch of their lives, is all influenced very strongly by pornography and to a lesser extent by celebrities posting selfies on social media.

Penis Size

Again boys' concerns about this are often directly connected to pornography. The actors who feature in these films are usually well-endowed for obvious reasons but what young men don't always know is that they frequently use various techniques to temporarily enlarge the penis and take drugs to maintain erections. All of this goes toward fuelling a very unhealthy obsession with this part of the male anatomy. It is just as demeaning to men as the widely accepted obsession with artificially enhanced breasts and the visual appearance of female genitals is to women. How many times do we hear on mainstream media, both in films and other programmes, the reference to 'does size matter?'? It infuriates me! Surely sex should be about caring for someone, fun, enjoyment, consideration, etc. Yet we still expound the myth that it is a purely physical thing. No wonder boys often feel inadequate. To add some balance to this view, try introducing the subject in a generalised way and certainly not in a way that is going to make your teenager feel uncomfortable. You could just react in the appropriate way when you hear the 'size matters' reference, saying what nonsense this is and that only people who don't know anything about the shared enjoyment of sex would hold this opinion. The fact is most penises are in and around 7 centimetres when flaccid and more or less double in size when erect. The length of a fully developed vagina is roughly

7 centimetres, a piece of information that often shocks both boys and girls.

As parents you will all have your own views on whether or not pornography is dangerous or just a bit of fun. Your attitude to this is very important. For instance, if you think pornography is harmful then you would probably be shocked and a little upset if your teenage children viewed it, but if you think it is just a bit of fun you may take a more relaxed stance. There is, however, an important difference in you watching pornography and your teenage son or daughter watching it and that is the degree to which you will be influenced by what you see. This is part of the reason why it carries an 18 cert.

If you are concerned about this it would probably be counter-productive to ask outright if your son or daughter watches pornography. You are unlikely to get a truthful answer and you have already raised their defences by asking what they will consider to be an intrusive question. You could try talking about the subject in a generalised way, maybe saying that you have read this book and ask them what they think about it. This has a couple of benefits. Firstly, you have broached a taboo subject and normalised it, and, secondly, you are asking their opinion therefore demonstrating that you value what they have to say. Don't use it as an excuse to lecture though. If they say something that is totally opposite to your belief just listen and challenge in such a way that it leads to more discussion and not to the closing down of the subject.

If you don't quite know how to start this conversation here are a few suggestions. But try to resist starting the conversation by giving your opinion of porn, especially if it is really negative, because this may inhibit your teenager from expressing their opinion. You could start by saying you have just read this book and there is a reference to the influence of pornography on young people. Then ask them:

- What do you think the main influences are? Are there positive and negative influences?
- Would you agree that it can influence body image, for both boys and girls?

- Do you think that young people are aware that it is just acting?
- What effect do you think it could have on a relationship?
- Would you agree that it should carry an 18 cert?

Obviously some teenagers will flatly refuse to engage with you on this and if this is the case LET IT DROP! Once it has ceased to be a two-way conversation it can develop into a bit of an inquisition and that is the last thing you want. If you are lucky and they do engage but their opinions are diametrically opposed to yours don't get the soapbox out. Just listen and then put your view forward. You may not change their opinion but at least you have engaged them in an actual conversation that hopefully has offered an opportunity to hear another point of view and they also now realise that if they do want to talk in the future you will be comfortable doing so.

SAFE SEX

Obviously when talking to your teenagers about sexual feelings and sexual activity it is important to address the whole area of safe sex and the need for young people to protect themselves from both unwanted pregnancy and infection.

Condoms are still the contraceptive of choice for many young people. This choice is mainly influenced by availability, price and the fact that no doctor's appointments are necessary. Both boys and girls should be encouraged to be responsible as far as contraception is concerned, particularly if they find themselves in an unplanned sexual situation. Probably not what you would hope for, but at least they will be protected if they have condoms with them *and they know how to use them!* They should familiarise themselves with this before they are in a situation where they need them. Here are some basics:

- Buy a reputable brand and make sure they are in date.
- Never open the packet with your teeth (this can tear the condom).

- Put the condom on the penis before any contact with the genitals.
- When putting the condom on hold the teat between the finger and the thumb and roll the condom up the penis to the top.
- After ejaculation hold the condom onto the penis during withdrawal.
- Do not use a lube as this can react with the latex.
- If possible, spermicide should be used in conjunction with the condom as extra protection against pregnancy (this is more likely when sex is part of a relationship).

Other important factors:

- The only form of contraception that also offers any protection against STIs are barrier contraceptives such as condoms or femidoms (female condom). The pill, implant, diaphragm, IUD or injection offer no protection against STIs.
- Condoms should also be used when performing oral sex as a number of STIs can also infect the mouth and throat. Many STIs can also cause infection in the eyes and some of these infections can be serious and hard to treat.
- Women who have sex with women are considered to be the least at risk of STIs but that does not mean it can't happen, so the same rules should apply about knowledge of sexual history. A dental dam is a barrier that can be placed over the female genitals during cunnilingus (oral sex with a female); they can be bought in a chemist or made by cutting open a condom.
- Anal sex carries more risk of infection than vaginal penetration. This risk is from infection through anal secretions and the possible tearing of the skin that lines the anus. Anal sex is more likely to take place between men who have sex with men but not solely. It is also a choice with some heterosexual couples and possibly due to the influence of pornography it is becoming more of

a mainstream choice for some people. It is, however, often one of the activities that girls feel pressured into participating in against their wishes.

There are of course other forms of contraception available and information is readily available from the IFPA (Irish Family Planning Association), Well Woman clinics, doctors' surgeries or online. Should you and your daughter opt for hormonal contraception (the pill, bar, patch or injection) she should have a full medical and discuss the pros and cons with a medical professional such as her family doctor or the IFPA. She should also be reminded that unless she is fully aware of the sexual history of the other party she should not indulge in unprotected sex without a condom.

CONSENT

By the time our children reach their teenage years they should already have a good understanding of what consent means. Some useful ways to introduce this to children were covered in Chapter 9.

As parents we may need to remind our teenage children that where sexual contact is concerned 'no' means 'no', and it is not an invitation to try harder! Unfortunately, this attitude has been perpetuated by film and other kinds of media. When I was a teenager a lot of films depicted the sexually aggressive male getting what he wanted from the sometimes reluctant 'weaker' females who were often secretly pleased by this 'manly' behaviour. Well we have moved on a little from this attitude but I am afraid it still prevails to some extent. Even among young people who should know better, not to mention some not-so-young people who also should know better. There is a little bit of nature and nurture at play here; the old 'Caveman Syndrome' is alive and well, and add to this the unreal expectation between both peers and the older generation that all teenagers are probably sexually active and it can be minefield to negotiate for anybody, let alone the young.

When talking to teens about consent it is paramount to point out that the absence of a 'yes' or any sign of reluctance should be deemed as a 'no'. We have to be careful not to demonise boys as far as consent is concerned as I believe that the vast majority of them have good intentions, so once again education and good communication is the key. As parents we should stress that for their sake and the sake of the girl they need to clarify the fact that she is willing and this willingness should be established at each point of sexual activity.

We obviously also need to speak to girls about personal responsibility - not to knowingly put themselves into situations that would compromise their safety such as leaving a club with somebody they have just met, accepting a lift from somebody they don't know or drinking so much alcohol that their judgement is impaired or they are incapable of looking after themselves. At the same time they should be told that they are entitled to call a stop to sexual activity at any point, but it is a good idea to make their views known about where they stand on sexual contact at the outset. When this suggestion is made to teenagers they are inclined to think it is funny or a bit weird. Their usual response is 'how would you bring the subject up?' Well I have to agree it could be a bit awkward but better feel a little awkward than for a situation to get out of hand. Reading and sending signals is something some people do with ease but not everybody is as adept so you can give the following pointers:

- If you meet someone that you like and you want to kiss them don't put yourself in a situation where this might get out of hand, e.g. by going somewhere private with them.
- If you are comfortable with the sexual interaction up to a point but you feel that you are having to control the situation because they are getting carried away either stop or just say 'I am not comfortable with that' or 'we need to stop now'.

- Encourage your teenager to feel happy with their comfort zone and not feel that they have to make excuses for their beliefs or attitudes.

The issue of boys feeling pressured into sexual activity is also important and boys need to be supported in their right to say 'no'. It isn't as common for boys to find themselves under pressure but it does happen and some girls can be sexually aggressive, especially when alcohol is involved. So talk to your son basically the same way as you would talk to your daughter: they don't have to do anything they feel uncomfortable about, they should excuse themselves and leave if they feel things are getting out of hand, and they should be confident enough to say 'I just don't want to have sex with you.'

Unwholesome and unhealthy attitudes to sexual behaviour will not vanish overnight but the more open we can be about rights, expectations, hopes and possible worries surrounding sex the more chance there is of our teenage children having a healthier view of it.

As previously mentioned, drink sometimes plays a part in non-consensual sex. I learned a very valuable lesson regarding this as a young teenager. My parents had agreed to me having a party for my sixteenth birthday and had also very reluctantly agreed to absent themselves for a few hours. There was no drink allowed at the party but a number of people had been drinking before they arrived, including a couple of girls I barely knew who were friends of friends. One of these girls, who was somebody I had only met a couple of times and was quietly envious of due to her good looks and seemingly endless supply of beautiful clothes, threw up shortly after she arrived. My sister and I got her to the bathroom, cleaned her up and put her on my bed to sleep it off. After a while I went in to check on her and found a boy, whom I also hardly knew, lying on the bed next to the sleeping girl with the front zip of her dress open. I asked him what he thought he was doing and told him to get out of the house. She was unaware of what had happened until I told her and she was really upset to think that if I had not checked on her when I did something more serious might have happened.

All of this was before #MeToo or any other publicity regarding consent; in fact I can honestly say the word was hardly uttered when I was a teenager. There had certainly been no publicised cases of girls, high-profile or otherwise, going to the authorities to complain about such incidents, and if they had all responsibility would probably have been laid very firmly at their feet anyway. It would very definitely have been a case of people tut-tutting and remarking that she should be ashamed for allowing herself to get into that state. As I said, it was a very valuable lesson to me at quite a young age and if anything it probably contributed to my slightly over-zealous attitude where drink is involved. But better safe than sorry.

Well here we are in the twenty-first century and thankfully attitudes have changed. Or have they? I am afraid there is still an onus on the victim to prove that they did not give consent and some people still believe that if the victim is not physically hurt then they must have either given consent or at least didn't mind that much. The fact is most people who are placed in the position of forced sexual intercourse don't put up a physical fight. This may be due to the fact that they were not conscious or completely conscious, they may just feel that they would be in more danger by putting up a fight, or it could be that they simply freeze with fear. The fact is if the person is not coherent enough to give consent that is a 'NO'. This applies whether the victim is male or female.

Rape within relationships is unfortunately not uncommon. I have spoken to girls who said that they have 'friends' who were reluctant to say no to their boyfriend because they would get moody with them or even occasionally threaten them or physically force them. This kind of behaviour very frequently goes unreported because the victim is romantically involved with the perpetrator. In fact, the victims often do not see their partner as a perpetrator and occasionally even justify their actions by taking on responsibility for causing the incident by being unloving and refusing sexual contact. It is important to remember that just because a person has agreed to have sex with you once they have not automatically agreed to have sex with you at any other time in the future. Likewise, if a couple have sex before going asleep that does not mean that there is an unwritten agreement that sex will be on the menu for breakfast.

Sex should always be seen as something to be enjoyed by both parties, equally fulfilling to both and not used as a bargaining tool or a reward for good behaviour, because it is then seen as something that is more important to one person in the relationship than the other and thus creates inequality.

When speaking to teenagers and discussing this issue they were sometimes amused that I should suggest asking permission of the other party before touching any part of their body that is considered to be private. For instance if a boy and girl are kissing passionately it does not automatically follow that she would be agreeable to having her breasts touched, or if she is okay with this that there is a green light to touch her genitals. It is always safer and more respectful if permission is sought before progressing to any intimate touching. Equally, it should not be automatically assumed that a boy wants to be touched sexually, even if they are obviously aroused. We need to encourage open, respectful communication about sex and to do this we as parents need to find and understand our own comfort zone.

One thing you can do as parents is watch a short video on YouTube called 'Tea and Consent' and after viewing it you could either suggest your teenage sons and daughters watch it or watch it together. It is a humorous way of getting across a very important point.

UNPLANNED PREGNANCY

I think this is a positive concern unlike some of the previous concerns. Both boys and girls need to be cognisant of this possibility. However this concern does not always stop them taking chances. Both boys and girls are probably more concerned about the risk of pregnancy if it is a one-night stand as opposed to a relationship. Most teenagers think they are quite responsible as far as contraception is concerned but unfortunately in the case of unplanned sex contraception is not always available – a fact which very rarely acts as a deterrent, again particularly if alcohol is involved. Not all teenagers decide to have sex even when under the influence of alcohol; some make a conscious decision to not have sex at all whilst others may just indulge in heavy petting or oral sex, behaviour that is quite common in older teenagers. The fact is, though, that teenagers are risk-takers which is why some of them drink too much, smoke cigarettes, use drugs and drive too fast. Of course not all of them can be accused of these things but it is generally accepted to be true of a lot of them. When we are young we are inclined to think that bad things only happen to other people. I can remember this feeling as I am sure you can. Luckily, I managed to get through my teenage years with nothing more than a smoking habit (since ditched) but that was probably due more to good luck than good behaviour.

As I mentioned earlier, teenagers are at the mercy of Mother Nature and she has lots of tricks up her sleeve to get them to have sex and become parents. There are very few teenagers not interested in kissing. A fairly harmless activity in itself but the reason we enjoy kissing so much is that it stimulates an erogenous zone, releases hormones and pheromones, and generally relaxes us. This leads to heightened sexual excitement, which is why kissing is a very important part of foreplay and often leads to other more serious sexual behaviour. So even though in the cold light of day your teenager understands that sex carries risks, when they are caught up in the heat of the moment it can be very hard to exercise control, which is why they should be prepared before they find themselves in the situation. Parents are sometimes reluctant to suggest this in case they appear to be encouraging such behaviour but it is as unlikely that your teenager will be encouraged to have sex because of having this conversation as they would be discouraged to have sex because their parents have told them they shouldn't. You can, of course, tell your teenager that you would prefer they wouldn't be sexually active for your given reasons, but refusing to address the topic by burying your head in the sand or telling them 'to keep it in their trousers' is pointless.

17

Intimacy

Teenagers can get any amount of information about the practicalities of sex at the click of a button but what they have much less access to is an insight into the whole area of intimacy. Some of them have never even heard the word. This is really unfortunate as sex without intimacy, whether it is between the young or not-so-young, can be emotionally damaging and stands much less chance of being fulfilling. Many people in search of intimacy and closeness confuse this need with sexual contact and may find themselves having generally unsatisfactory sex with multiple partners because they are using sex as a shortcut to intimacy, which very rarely, if ever, works out.

Parents sometimes find the subject of intimacy tricky to approach, possibly because they have never really given it much thought themselves or maybe because they find the conversation too awkward as it can be connected to sexual pleasure and they do not want to appear to be encouraging their children to become sexually active. Whether it is for these or other reasons it is a subject very rarely touched on.

A few questions that parents might suggest their teenagers consider before becoming sexually active are:

- *Do I feel safe in this relationship and is there mutual trust?*
  Sometimes teenagers think that sexual activity increases
  closeness and trust but if these qualities are not there in
  the first place sex can have the opposite effect.
- *Do I understand the implications of sex in a relationship
  and have I discussed these with my partner?*
  A good exercise is to discuss what they think might
  be improved about their relationship if they decide to
  have sex, what if anything might be dis-improved, and
  what are the wider risks. If two people are not comfortable talking about sex openly they are not ready for the
  commitment of a sexual relationship.
- *Why do I want to have sex with this person at this time?*
  If the answer to this is more about pleasing a partner or
  feeling pressured into 'going along with it' for whatever
  reason then this is not a good idea. Neither is it a good
  idea to have sex because all of your friends are having
  sex. I have even heard on more than one occasion 'well
  you have to lose your virginity at some time'. The first
  time somebody has sex should be discussed practically and emotionally by the couple and if either one of
  them feels pressured it shouldn't happen. It should be a
  special moment with mutual care and respect.

Of course not all intimacy is sexual intimacy, so parents could
explore the aspect of intimacy with regard to being totally
yourself with another person and not having to pretend to
be something or somebody you aren't or the knowledge that
the love you share is not incumbent on you doing what your
partner wants you to do.

A good exercise for parents would be to define intimacy for
yourself, ask your partner to do the same and then compare
notes. You might be surprised and you might not, but what
this exercise will almost certainly do is open up an interesting
conversation which will hopefully be helpful when talking to
your teenagers.

The following real-life case study provides a clear illustra-
tion of how sex and intimacy can often be confused.

A few years ago I received a phone call from a teacher I had become friendly with in the course of my work. She told me that a friend of hers was very concerned about her teenage daughter. According to the girl's mother she was 'going off the rails'. My friend asked me to contact them to see if I could be of any help as the mother was 'at her wits' end' and didn't really know how to address what was happening. When I called the mother she was extremely distressed. Apparently she had been concerned about her daughter for a few months but all attempts to get to the bottom of her behaviour had been met with the old stonewalling technique – which is very predictable teenage behaviour, as any parent will tell you. It all came to a head when she got a call from the Gardaí to say that her daughter had been picked up in a park with a couple of boys smoking weed. The mother decided it was time to stop pussyfooting about and when her daughter went to school the next morning she went in search of her diary, which was something that she never thought she would do. But, as she said, desperate times call for desperate measures. What she read completely shocked her and a part of her wished that she hadn't read it all. Her daughter had made a list of all of her sexual partners and the behaviour that had taken place with them. Now that the mother had this information she didn't quite know what to do with it and she asked me would I be agreeable to meet them both and facilitate a conversation. I said I would, providing the daughter was happy with this. She was, so we arranged to meet in a coffee shop and after a while the mother left us to chat alone. When the mother had gone I asked the daughter what was happening in her life, particularly in connection with boys and the behaviour as outlined in her diary. She said she didn't really know why she was doing it. I asked her was she getting any enjoyment out of it and she said 'no'. To get a more complete picture I asked her when she had first had sex and she told me that it was on her sixteenth birthday with her then boyfriend. She didn't feel ready for it but they had been together for two years and he was putting pressure on her by saying that all of his friends were having sex and they were giving him a hard time because he was the only one in a relationship and the only one apparently not having sex. She didn't really enjoy it when it happened but she wanted to please him because she loved him and believed he loved her. However, when he ended the relationship a couple of months later she was totally heartbroken and felt like she had lost her soul mate – a very normal reaction to the ending of your first serious relationship.

Her friends rallied around and did what friends do best with the old 'you're too good for him' conversation and endless phone calls rehashing what happened. After a couple of weeks of moping about she agreed to go to a disco with them, encouraged by her mum as she thought it would help her get over her ex. She met a boy she vaguely knew and after a while he asked her to go outside with him where they kissed and when he asked her for oral sex she agreed. The attention made her feel better than she had felt since the break-up and when he said he would be in touch she was really happy and expected to hear from him. When she didn't hear from him she was a bit down but expected to see him the next time she went to the disco – which she did but unfortunately wrapped around another girl. She wasn't too disappointed because as she was a really good-looking girl she was getting quite a lot of male attention. She was asked to go outside with another boy and she found herself in a similar situation. Although it wasn't really what she wanted she was flattered by the attention. She started getting messages from various boys she didn't even know. These messages were generally complimentary and the fact that she seemed to be so popular all of a sudden made her feel good. Her reputation took a bit of a battering with some of the girls she thought were her friends and pretty soon she was being 'slut-shamed' not only within her group of so-called friends but also at school. As you know, salacious gossip travels very quickly! This was really hurtful for her, especially as she was already coping with the break-up of her relationship. In the meantime her number was being shared among a particular group of boys who were encouraging her to hang out with them and telling her what she wanted to hear whilst in return she was giving them what they wanted sexually.

When I asked her what she was getting out of it she said 'nothing'. I said 'so why are you doing it?' To this she just shrugged and looked upset. I asked her what she would really like to happen and she said she just wanted one of them not to want to have sex with her and just hang out with her, watching a movie or going for a walk. We talked further about how she could take back the power and not wait for one of the boys to tell her that it was okay not to have sex. What she needed was to love and respect herself and then other people would treat her the way she deserved to be treated.

What she was searching for was intimacy, not sex. She wanted someone to see her for who she was and to want to spend time with her. In short, she wanted the relationship she had had with her boyfriend before it became sexual, but she was using sex to try to take a shortcut to this. This is not uncommon as when people have had sex in a previous relationship and that relationship ends they are more likely to become sexual at an earlier stage in subsequent relationships. This is more likely to happen when a relationship has ended badly, leaving one person nursing a broken heart.

I suggested that she spend more time at home for a while with her family, ignore the gossips and not make any further arrangements with boys. I also suggested that she have a look at her friendships and sort out the real friends from the fake. As any adult knows there will be someone new to talk about tomorrow. She said she would try to do this and as this girl had the support of her parents and some real friends I was fairly confident that she would get the desired outcome, but not everybody is so lucky.

If this kind of behaviour goes unnoticed or accepted as the norm it can occasionally become habitual and lead to emotional problems that are often exacerbated by other people's attitudes. If people are being sexual as part of an intimate relationship they are far more likely to have fulfilling, enjoyable sex and therefore less likely to have multiple partners. After all why would you change your partner if you are having a satisfying relationship? So although it is not always the case, people who have sex with multiple partners are sometimes doing so in search of intimacy and of being seen and valued for who they are, which is after all what an intimate relationship is about. They blame their dissatisfaction with these liaisons on the other person and enter into an endless and fruitless search for 'the one' who will make them feel good but as long as they are using sex as a shortcut to finding this it will probably never happen.

Reassurance is what teenagers need in these circumstances, not judgement, so if as parents you are concerned about an aspect of your teenager's behaviour try not to finger-wag or talk about shame because they are possibly already feeling some shame and it will be counterproductive to add to this in any way. Remember what we should be encouraging is for our children to develop a positive attitude towards themselves, to reinforce their right to be treated respectfully and lovingly, and to not confuse casual sex with intimacy.

The pursuit of intimacy should not be mistaken as the sole preserve of girls. A number of years ago I arrived at a school in a fairly disadvantaged area and was asked to take a small group of students who had been segregated from the main group due to behavioural problems. I was told that they may or may not last the morning and if they should get bored or restless to let them leave, and was told where they should report to if this was the case. The group consisted of five girls and three boys. On arrival in the classroom I introduced myself and as an ice-breaker told them something I liked and something I didn't like and asked them to do the same. To say they were resistant is an understatement but with encouragement they reluctantly agreed to tell me their name and something they liked and something they disliked. The first girl gave me her name and she said 'I like my mates and hate two-faced c**ts!' I asked her was she one, to which she indignantly replied 'no'. I said that this was probably not strictly true as we are all two-faced at times and asked her what she thought life would be like if we were always totally honest. She started to laugh at the prospect of this and said we would probably kill each other. This lightened the atmosphere in the group and they started to relax as they could see I was not shockable or there to chastise them.

As always, I asked them what they would like to talk about and the only suggestion from all eight of them was sex. I told them that if I was just going to talk about sex the workshop would be very short so I asked them did anybody know what intimacy was and they all said that they had never heard of it. I went on to describe intimacy as I understood it by saying 'It is when somebody really sees you and by that I mean the *real* you, not the physical you. It is when you know that whatever you have with them is special and will not be shared with anybody else; if you have sex with them you don't have to ask yourself what they think of you because you already know and you don't have to wonder will you see them again later, or tomorrow or the next day because you are a part of their lives.'

As I was saying this I noticed that the girl who made the two-faced c**ts remark was wiping her eye and the girl sitting next to her said 'are you crying?' I asked her was she alright and she said 'yeah it's just what you're saying sounds lovely.' I said 'it is lovely. Is that what you would like in a relationship?' To which she nodded. I asked the other girls would they also like this and they said 'yes'. With that a boy who up to this point had said nothing at all slammed his hand down on the desk and said 'but that's what we want too but boys are just afraid to say it in case they [gesturing to the girls] laugh at them!' I asked the other boys in the group if they agreed and they said they did. The girls were quite shocked and challenged them on this and they had one of the most honest exchanges between students that I ever witnessed in the course of my work.

I have used both of these examples when working with other groups of teenagers, who are often more than a little surprised to hear that boys require intimacy just as much as girls, which might sometimes be overlooked due to conditioning, stereotypes and the suit of armour that is donned by a lot of young and not-so-young men.

Mental Health Issues

18

It could be argued that it is a positive development that the topic of mental health issues is raised for discussion more than it used to be. Hopefully this means that young people are more aware and more comfortable to talk about it, and not that it is becoming more common. I, however, suspect it is a bit of both.

Social media is one of the reasons why this topic is being highlighted more. There are more fora for young people to discuss mental health issues, which is good, but I do worry that sometimes it can exacerbate a problem that could be dealt with more effectively by the person involved having a face-to-face conversation with a relative, a teacher or even a friend. I also worry that there is a growing inclination to label certain behaviours as mental health problems such as phobias, OCD, etc. I would be a rich woman if I got a Euro for every time I heard a student in a classroom or somebody on the television referring to something that they do not like as a phobia: 'I've got a phobia of cheese' or 'I've got a phobia of someone scraping their nails on a particular surface.' These are not phobias – you just don't like them. Equally, teenagers refer to certain behaviours either in themselves or their friends as OCD: 'she has OCD when it comes to applying makeup' or 'I have OCD about brushing my teeth properly.' Well as long as you are not brushing your teeth excessively during the day it probably just means that you like clean teeth. It is not hugely worrying but it might just minimise an actual problem when it is spoken about like this.

Some issues such as self-harm can become quite fashionable in the school community, as can eating disorders. I am not attempting to trivialise either of these phenomena but I have noticed that where you get one case of a student self-harming in a school you can sometimes get a number of classmates presenting with the same problem. It is of course not only worrying but quite distressing, whether it is just a copycat situation or not, and it needs to be dealt with – but I feel it is worth noting that these problems are very rarely isolated incidents. If you as a parent become aware of a problem with your child you should obviously seek help from your GP to ensure the right regime of treatment, but you should also inform your child's school and suggest that they get professional help from the relevant body to address the situation. This may involve inviting a speaker from the organisation concerned to visit the school to speak to staff and students, or discussions on mental health could be incorporated into an SPHE lesson. It might also be worth speaking to the parents of your child's close friends to alert them that there is possibly a problem within the group of friends. I understand that this may be difficult for you as mental health problems are a very private issue, but it is just another illness that may be contagious so try to treat it this way. After all, if your child had chickenpox you would inform the parents of their friends to alert them to possible symptoms and this is not that different.

Another noticeable issue is the over-obsession with appearance. The amount of young people considering cosmetic surgery, botox and fillers is growing. Very few people share undoctored pictures of themselves on social media. Their attitude is that everybody else does it so if they share a warts-and-all picture they are at a disadvantage. What this is doing is adding substance to the belief that we need to conform to whatever is the present standard of unrealistic manufactured 'beauty'. Is it any wonder that eating disorders and body dysmorphia are more common now than they have ever been? This is a difficult problem for parents to deal with as it is quite innocuous and frequently goes under the radar. I am not suggesting that there is a need to over-analyse the behaviour of your teenage children. It is normal for them to become more interested in their appearance and to pay more attention to what others think of them. For some people this can continue into adulthood, but luckily for most of us our self-esteem becomes less vulnerable the older we get and we learn to accept ourselves for who we are.

The difference between the normal level of 'obsession' demonstrated by a lot of teenagers and an actual problem is if your child becomes anxious or depressed about their appearance, imagining problems that aren't there and honing in on their body shape or one of their features and insisting they need surgery to combat an imaginary fault. A young person who is experiencing problems in this area may also start to lose touch with friends because they feel inadequate in their company and they can at times either show reluctance to shop for new clothes or be overly critical when trying them on.

What might be helpful as a parent is to be realistic whilst still being positive. For instance, if your child is self-conscious about their weight and there is good reason for this concern it is not helpful for you to say 'there is nothing wrong with you. You suit being curvy' and then give them a hot chocolate to make them feel better. Neither would it be helpful for you to constantly remind them of their weight problem. Instead you could listen to what they say and tell them that if they aren't happy they can adjust their diet and do more exercise. When I say 'adjust their diet' this does not mean a crash diet or a fad diet; it means eating a well-balanced diet, maybe with smaller portions. I would throw out the bathroom scales; they are not needed. If your teenager is eating well and getting enough exercise it doesn't matter what the scales say. Finally, whatever the problem, imaginary or otherwise, you should listen to what is being said and if you think there are grounds for concern look into this together and let your child know you support them.

Having said all of this, growing up as a child in a mainly female household with a mother and three older sisters, it was a normal part of life for me to observe them applying makeup, doing their hair, paying attention to their weight, etc. and this definitely impacted on the way I saw myself as a young woman. I never even considered not wearing makeup and as soon as I was able to buy some I did. It was very cheap and badly applied, I might add. My mother and my sisters all coloured their hair so once again it was completely natural for me to follow suit. None of this was particularly harmful, or at least not as far as I can see other than to make us all slightly superficial in some ways - a trait I have since tried hard to correct. The difference between attitudes then and now however is poles apart. I didn't have strangers examining a photograph of me and posting their opinions online; I didn't have bloggers demonstrating contouring and promoting cosmetic procedures. There was no such thing as online trolls whose only purpose in life is to hurt or dent the self-esteem of anyone they feel deserves it, which translates as anyone who puts themselves out there. So is it any wonder this generation of young people has more noticeable issues in this area than previous generations?

If we can find ways of encouraging our children to look beneath the surface it would be the first step in them developing more realistic attitudes to personal appearance so they are more likely to be interested in what a person *is* like, not what they *look* like. Encourage them to embrace diversity and individualism as far as possible. The best way to do this is by mirroring. We should choose the language used when talking about somebody carefully: do not always comment either positively or adversely on someone's weight or fashion sense or physical appearance. Instead comment on what they say or do if at all possible. Obviously it is occasionally necessary to describe someone's physical appearance but it should not always be the first port of call when talking about someone. If we remember to do this we are giving our children a very clear message that looks or appearance are not of primary importance.

Sometimes parents ask what are the warning signs for mental health problems. Well this can differ from person to person. For one person spending a lot of time in their bedroom and being uncommunicative with parents is just being a normal teenager, but for another it could be the sign of a possible problem. As a general rule of thumb if your teenager's behaviour changes fairly suddenly, they stop going out or talking to friends, their eating habits change and they either start to eat a lot more or a lot less, or insisting on eating in their bedroom, or they are becoming lethargic and disinterested it might be a good idea to have a word with the school counsellor or year head to check if they have noticed anything. Try to broach the subject gently and not be too alarmist; if you continue to be concerned have a word with your family doctor.

As parents we want our children to be happy and loved. A normal enough aspiration you might say. Well it is equally normal that they will at times be unhappy and not loved by everyone. If we can be realistic with our children and not treat them like hothouse flowers they will be better equipped to deal with the more negative things that life throws at them on a daily basis. It would seem that my parents' generation were more critical and less complimentary than my generation of parents. I got very few if any compliments from my mother or father and was told about my shortcomings fairly regularly, as were my other siblings. From conversations with friends of the same age it appears that they received similar treatment and this may have caused my generation of parents to be overprotective, slightly pushy and unrealistically effusive with their children, with the smallest of criticisms regarding one of our children seen as a major insult. We should, of course, strive for the happy medium. Compliments and encouragement are good but we need to be realistic. The occasional critical observation is healthy and keeps us grounded. Our children are not perfect any more than we are. They will be liked by some people, loved by fewer people and hopefully disliked by fewer still.

For those parents who feel that their relationship with their teenage children has broken down irreparably I would like to

offer some comfort. Very few stroppy, uncommunicative teenagers grow into stroppy, uncommunicative adults, and this is
not because their parents have murdered them. It is because of
a little matter of independence and space, both of which will
happen eventually. When they start to need us less and some
of the responsibility shifts from us to them they may start to
see us as actual people rather than jailers and this leads to a
more open and honest relationship. Finally, learn to pick your
battles. Not all arguments and emotional upsets are caused
by teenagers so be honest with yourself about your expectations of them and the way in which you deal with difficult
situations.

The Effect of Drugs and Drink on Relationships

19

Whilst it is true that the misuse of alcohol and drugs is more common in the younger generation it is certainly not true that this applies to all young people. Most teenagers will relate to drinking enough to make themselves sick but this is not necessarily done with regularity. It can be an isolated occurrence for a lot of them and although they may continue to drink alcohol they generally try to avoid a repeat performance. There are those, though, who don't seem either to learn or maybe care about the effect of drinking too much and look on severe hangovers or more serious side-effects as a byproduct of enjoying themselves. I have spoken to young people who will throw up due to alcohol consumption but continue to drink afterwards. But then I also know some adults capable of this kind of behaviour. I have lost count of the number of students who say 'what's the point of drinking if you aren't going to get drunk?' So how do young people see drink affecting their relationships?

As anybody who drinks knows, one of the effects of alcohol consumption can be the 'frog/prince' phenomenon and because we are talking about people who are already at the mercy of Mother Nature even the most dubious-looking frog can become attractive to them if they have had enough to drink. In some cases it is just a case of kissing somebody you would normally not even say hello to, which at worse is just embarrassing, but in other cases the situation goes further with some young people engaging in one-night stands or even public sexual acts. This usually leads to huge regret by the person involved, followed by shame and sometimes depression.

It might be useful as parents to have a quiet conversation with your son or daughter when they reach the age of going out with friends to clubs and so on. Offering practical advice is more useful than just warning them not to get drunk. You could try suggesting that for every alcoholic drink they have they should follow it with a non-alcoholic one. For instance, if they are drinking vodka and coke (a favourite apparently) they could just leave the vodka out for every alternate drink. This halves the amount of alcohol they consume. Be specific about your concerns, which are probably the frog/prince phenomenon, danger of not being in control, anger and violence (usually involving more young men than young women), physical dangers such as alcohol poisoning, and the possibility of drink-related accidents such as pedestrian and traffic accidents.

Occasionally when two people are in a relationship and one or both of them starts to drink to excess or use drugs the impact on the relationship can be quite serious, sometimes resulting in violence, cheating, lack of trust and loyalty, etc. It can also result in the person who does not drink or use drugs becoming very anxious when they are out together, never quite knowing what will happen, will their girlfriend/boyfriend get into an argument or a physical fight, either with them or with somebody else, or will they be asked to leave a club or bar because they are being too loud or aggressive.

So how can you help your children to recognise a problem and deal with it sensibly? Firstly, by not preaching. Teenagers have an automatic off switch when parents use a preachy tone of voice. If you have noticed something you are concerned about, either in your own child or their boyfriend or girlfriend, be clear about what you want to say before you say anything. Then just state your observations, make sure they are accurate and don't exaggerate them. If it is your child tell them why you are concerned – health, safety, emotional wellbeing, etc. – ask them to be honest about the amount they are drinking, and get some factual information leaflets about safe levels of alcohol. If the problem is not your child but their boyfriend or girlfriend talk to them about how they feel about the issue. Are they worried? What are their worries, etc.? Recommend that they are honest with their boyfriend/girlfriend about their concerns and recommend that they ask them to try to reduce their level of alcohol consumption, and if they are having difficulty complying with this they need to leave the relationship and inform the parent(s) of the person involved.

Teenagers are less likely to be honest about their use of illegal drugs than alcohol. There are some teenagers who would never be tempted to use drugs at all but unfortunately there are others who are more open to experimentation. A lot of it depends on the company they keep. If their friends use drugs socially they are more likely to use them. Mostly they will survive their teenage years relatively unscathed by this but it does depend on the drugs they use, how often they use them and the amount they use, their personality type and family history. When speaking to students most of them would say that they would never want a boyfriend or girlfriend who used drugs. When asked for their reasons their usual response is that they just don't want to be around someone who uses drugs because it is dangerous, illegal and they act in an erratic way. They also do not want an addict in their life. All of which is very valid. Of course not everybody who uses drugs becomes addicted but it is the possible outcome for anybody who dabbles in drug use. Drug users are frequently very selfish with little consideration for the people in their lives, which thankfully a lot of young people seem to be aware of.

If you are concerned that your child or the person they are involved with is using drugs you should get help to deal with the problem effectively. There are a number of free booklets from the HSE that will give you some insight into dealing with the problem. 'Alcohol and Drugs: A Parent's Guide' is full of useful information and can be downloaded by visiting www. askaboutalcohol.ie/parents/. There are also some very useful helplines available, such as Spunout.ie (Freephone 1800 459 459), Crosscare (01 836 0011) and Aware (1800 804 848).

Unplanned Pregnancy

20

Unplanned pregnancy is not just the girl's problem but whilst boys in relationships usually say they would shoulder half the burden if their girlfriend becomes pregnant, in the case of a one-night stand or casual sex they are generally far more reluctant to shoulder any responsibility. Thankfully, it is true that there is much less stigma attached to an unplanned pregnancy than in previous generations but, this being said, it is still many parents' worst nightmare. The attitude amongst girls varies quite a lot, from those who think it would not be the worst thing that could happen to them to those who are terrified at the prospect, whereas most boys become weak at the very idea. So why is it that in the twenty-first century we still have so many unplanned pregnancies when condoms are readily available and there is easily accessible advice available on contraception from the IFPA, family doctors and many other sources? The answer, as discussed in earlier chapters, is quite simple. The temptation to explore sexually is very strong in teenagers, some more than others. They do not consider the risks involved logically; instead they persuade themselves that it will never happen to them. A similar mindset is involved with alcohol use, drug use, smoking, driving too fast, etc.

So let's look at the worst-case scenario. You have discussed contraception with your teenager and they have assured you either that they are not sexually active or that they are taking precautions, but you find yourself having that very conversation you have dreaded. It's all very well for me to tell you to stay calm and count to ten before saying anything when really you might feel like your head is exploding, but staying calm is exactly what you need to try to do. Try to imagine how hard this conversation is for your son or daughter. They have probably been dreading it for a while before plucking up the courage to speak to you, and the last thing they need is blame, recriminations, hysteria or ultimatums. It may not be the news you had hoped for but it can be dealt with more positively if a conversation can be had with all of the concerned parties - that is the couple and the two sets of parents. After all a pregnancy impacts on more lives than just the prospective parents and all solutions should be open for discussion. Just remember that what you see as the best solution is not necessarily how everybody else will view it. So you may have to be prepared to compromise. The first thing your child needs is support and to best support them you have to put your needs on hold, albeit temporarily. The following questions might be a help if you don't know where to start:

- How do they feel about it?
- If it is your daughter has she discussed it with the father of the child and how does he feel?
- If it is your son ask him what has been discussed with the girl?
- Who else has been informed, i.e. the other set of parents?
- What do they see as the next move forward?

By doing this you are handing the responsibility back to them, which is, after all, where it belongs. I am not suggesting that you do not have a right to an opinion or that you can't make suggestions, but by using the above questions you are gently reminding them that they need to handle this like adults, which involves examining calmly what is best for them, what is best for the baby and what is best for both families. They need to realistically evaluate how this pregnancy will impact on their lives, both positively and negatively, and the lives of those associated with them and get as much information about all of the options available to them as possible.

You also may need support so do not be afraid to ask for it. It may sound obvious but just talking to a close friend or family member can often help get your worries into perspective. Or if you have a good relationship with your family doctor you could seek advice from them. My Options is a helpline run by the HSE that offers a free counselling service from 9 a.m. to 9 p.m. Monday to Friday and medical advice 24 hours a day, 7 days a week. The freephone number is 1 800 828 010. Finally, please remember this is not the end of the world and whatever decision is reached it will be made easier for all concerned by communicating honestly about the needs of everyone, including you.

Toxic Friendships

Firstly, let me be clear that the term 'toxic friendship' is the term chosen by the students and not one suggested by me or other facilitators. This topic is raised more by girls than boys. That is not to say that boys do not have difficulty with friendships but they do seem to handle the difficulties differently. When given the opportunity to discuss this issue both with their peers and the facilitator the problems mentioned by students usually fall into one of the following categories:

- Boyfriend/girlfriend issues
- Jealousy
- Disloyalty
- Demanding behaviour
- Competitiveness

BOYFRIEND/GIRLFRIEND ISSUES

The boyfriend/girlfriend issue could be one friend spending too much time with a new boyfriend/girlfriend at the expense of the friendship. We have probably all been there and can empathise with both of the friends in this situation. As you know, when you are in the throes of a new relationship you can't get enough of the person and it can make you a bit selfish sometimes at the expense of relationships with family and friends. This is where good communication is important. If the friend who feels ignored can talk about their feelings and not just go into a sulk they have a better chance of resolving the problem. It is worth pointing out that friendships are organic, not static, and we have to be prepared to change with time and other outside influences. It is also helpful to reverse the roles and examine honestly how they feel they would react in the reverse role and then discuss this with the friend involved.

Sometimes it can be the slightly more serious issue of a friend dating an ex. There is an unwritten rule amongst friends that you do not date each other's exes. There of course is no logical reason behind this and the more level-headed among us might say this is nonsense but it does seem to cause a lot of bad feeling. You, as a parent, might agree with this or be of the mind that they are an ex, therefore up for grabs. I can see both points of view and I suppose it depends on why they are an ex, who did the 'dumping', if the friend still has feelings for them and how it is handled. I would always suggest that if there is an interest in a friend's ex then there should be a decent period of mourning before any liaison is considered and then the friend should be consulted before it proceeds. It all comes down to how strong the attraction is and how much the friendship is valued. We can't always have the best of both worlds.

Occasionally the problem might be that the friend and the boyfriend/girlfriend just don't get on. Sometimes friends can be very vocal about not liking a friend's boyfriend/girlfriend and this can cause a division of loyalty with the person in the relationship not being able to please either the friend or the boyfriend/girlfriend. This can cause a rift between friends if a compromise isn't reached. For instance if it is your child who is having a problem with a friend's boyfriend/girlfriend suggest that they firstly look at their dislike rationally and identify what it is that they perceive as the problem, or is it just a case of the green-eyed monster? If there is an actual identifiable problem then they can talk to their friend diplomatically about it. If they can't identify the problem but they 'just don't like them' maybe they are just feeling a little pushed out and they could talk to their friend about this – not in an accusatory way but calmly telling them the way they feel. If your child is the one who is guilty of neglecting a friend you could remind them that although romantic relationships are very exciting they can become all-consuming very quickly and they should also remember to nurture their other friendships. Ask them how would they feel if their friend suddenly dropped them like a hot potato? Short-sightedness unfortunately is one of the side-effects of infatuation.

JEALOUSY

If the issue is jealousy it can be quite hard to deal with. Firstly, it is not always obvious that this is the issue as it is very rare that a person would admit to this character trait. It often presents itself by the friend who is jealous behaving in such a way that it damages the self-esteem of their so-called friend. They do this sometimes by putdowns, sometimes in public, and they often try to pass this off as 'banter', which of course is rubbish; banter is meant to be good-humoured with no hidden agenda, whereas putting somebody down is the opposite. They often pick on minor defects and blow them out of proportion. I could go on but you probably get the picture. If the friend was always in jealous mode it would be easy to deal with and most people would just end the friendship, but that is not usually the case or else they wouldn't have become friends in the first place.

If your child is dealing with a jealous friend, suggest they take the friend aside and point out the offending behaviour to them calmly, using examples of incidents that have caused hurt. Often the jealous friend is unaware of their behaviour. Depending on how the conversation goes the friendship will either move on to a more comfortable and positive position or it will end. If the friendship does end reassure your child that whilst this is hurtful it is better than tolerating and enabling such behaviour in their friend.

DISLOYALTY

Disloyalty is a big no-no for most friendships or relationships. It is very closely tied in with trust and you cannot have a true friendship if you do not trust the person you are friends with. Occasionally there is a small breach of loyalty which can cause a minor argument, for instance if one friend tells the other a fairly minor secret and it is then shared with somebody else. This is usually resolvable and not uncommon. Some people are just bad at keeping secrets, that doesn't make the friendship 'toxic'. It usually just results in the person involved not sharing anything too weighty with them. However, if a friend is told something that is really important and asked specifically not to repeat it and that is not respected it can cause a major rift in the friendship. We know if we are good at keeping secrets or not and if we know that it isn't one of our strengths, be honest and suggest that you are not told anything really secret just in case you accidentally blab.

The disloyalty may also take other forms, such as intentionally leaving a friend out of a social occasion for whatever reason, or not being honest with them if you have some information that they should be made aware of. All of these examples have been raised with groups of students and once again communication and honesty is of key importance.

It is not easy for an adult and even more so for a child to deal with this situation constructively, but you can encourage your teenager to communicate openly and honestly with their friend about how their behaviour has hurt them. If their friend is a genuine friend they will listen and hopefully stop the offending behaviour. As parents we should always be aware that we are only being given one view of the problem so, hard as it may be, try to maintain at least a small degree of objectivity. I say this through experience. I have lost count of the number of times I gave advice to my children based on the report of some dreadful injustice perpetrated by one or more of their friends only to find out that it was a storm in a teacup and they were as inseparable as ever by the next day.

I talked at the beginning of this book about empathy and how we should encourage our children to be empathetic. If we have empathy we will at least try to understand how the other person feels. It doesn't always mean that we will take the right course of action but it does mean that we will think twice before taking an action that may hurt another.

DEMANDING BEHAVIOUR

Overly demanding friends can be a problem. Many people have demanding friends or at least friends who can have periods of being demanding. When things are going well we do not really notice this trait too much, but when we either have other issues going on in our lives or we have less time or space for some reason this can then become a problem. If a friend is going through a hard time it is not only kind but the right thing to do to give them a friendly ear, but if it is just a personality trait that they are overly demanding it can become tiresome. There are people who are more high-maintenance than others, and whether this is a romantic relationship or a friendship it is very hard to sustain. It is also one of the most difficult concerns to address because there is no nice way of saying 'you are inconsiderate of my feelings.' What can be done is to address the situation as it comes up. So, for instance, if your child's friend is demanding their attention about a problem they may be experiencing with a boyfriend yet again (very frequently the case with teenage friends), your child can just say something like 'we have talked about this before and there is really nothing new for me to say.' Hopefully the friend will get the message that your child is not going to indulge them yet again. If they do not take the hint suggest to your child that they may have to be more blunt and tell their friend that they also have worries occasionally and they would like their friend to be more considerate of this and not constantly expecting your child to listen to their problems.

COMPETITIVENESS

Friends who are constantly in competition can be a problem. A little competition between friends is normal, and not only amongst teenage friends; I know some adults who are permanently in competition. It only becomes a problem when the more competitive friend has to win at any cost. This might be with boys'/girls' attention, appearance, success, popularity or any other area you can think of. This usually has one of two effects – either the less competitive friend just stops competing at all or they argue a lot, often leading to the dissolution of the friendship. If your child is dealing with a very competitive friend I would usually suggest if that friend has other admirable qualities then it is worth your child trying to have a conversation with their friend about how their behaviour makes them feel, explaining that they don't want to lose their friendship. However, if the friendship does not have more positives than negatives I would suggest your child just explain to their friend that they find their behaviour irritating and they don't want to be friends any longer. It is worth noting that the more competitive friend is possibly less confident and may feel a little inferior to the less competitive friend. After all, if you are happy with who you are you don't have to keep proving you are the best.

* * *

Teenagers respond very well to learning new relationship skills and are usually grateful when they have been taken seriously and their problems discussed respectfully. I cannot say that it changes their lives but with every new set of skills we can master the better the chance we have going forward of dealing with problems as they arise and this lessens the chance of a friendship becoming toxic.

It is sometimes hard to remain logical when our child approaches us with a problem. This is because we love them and it is normal to be biased in their favour, but it is more useful for them if after reassuring them that we look at the problem clearly and then discuss the necessary skills for dealing with it. They are more likely to turn to us again in the future if they feel they have been given realistic advice.

Dealing with Conflict in Relationships

22

As you know, conflict is ever-present in life. For some people it is a normal part of life and although they may not enjoy it they take it in their stride, but for others it can be debilitating.

CONFLICT STYLES

It is useful for teenagers, and adults of any age for that matter, to firstly recognise their conflict style. By doing this it helps us to recognise how we play out our role when conflict arises and it also helps us to recognise what our beliefs about conflict are and where we get these beliefs. There are a number of conflict styles and I have outlined a few of the more common and easily identifiable below. See if you recognise yourself. It might also be useful to show this list to your teenager and ask them what they think their style is. Of course you may be a mix of different styles and the predominant style can change with age, circumstances, etc.

Volcano

This person explodes without warning. A lot of teenagers will identify as this. You may even have one or two of them in your family. The volcano erupts sometimes with very little or no provocation and they have little regard for anyone caught in the eruption. This style is not usually productive or considerate of the other person's point of view. They usually feel spent after eruption and some of them at least will go away and reflect on what happened, and if not apologise maybe look for a way forward. There are volcanoes, however, who are just in a permanent state of eruption without any reflection afterwards. This can be very difficult to be around and very difficult for the volcano themselves.

Never confront a volcano during an eruption. It is usually safest and more productive to speak to them immediately afterwards as they are sometimes embarrassed by their behaviour and maybe feeling contrite. Try to explain how you feel when they erupt, using 'I' messages. For instance, 'I feel quite threatened when you shout', *not* 'you are threatening me', or 'I feel really hurt when you speak to me like that', *not* 'you are so hurtful speaking to me like that' – a small difference but a very important one. Your feelings are valid and you should be allowed to express them; remember nobody can argue with the way you feel. One last tip: do not say 'you make me feel' because that is still apportioning blame and may result in an escalation of the argument.

Ostrich

The ostrich buries their head and pretends nothing is wrong. Fewer teenagers fit into this category, as I am sure you can imagine. The ostrich hates confrontation and will do their best to avoid it. They usually stay out of trouble, both in school and at home, but the worrying thing about the ostrich is they are less likely to have their needs met. Going forward into more serious relationships the ostrich can actually cause conflict because the other person in the relationship may feel exasperated and angry at their incapacity to discuss a problem and therefore reach a resolution. Occasionally the ostrich will erupt just like the volcano, spraying all and sundry with feathers. Not a pretty sight. If you are an ostrich set yourself the challenge of confronting a problem that affects you. Start with a minor one if possible, maybe just saying something like 'I don't like it when you dismiss my opinion/are late, etc.' You will see the world won't fall apart. If you are involved with an ostrich try to consult them about decisions and don't let them away with saying 'whatever you think' or 'I really don't mind' – at least not all of the time.

Sulker

The sulker is very common. They also may refuse to discuss the problem rationally and productively, and choose to withdraw from the person involved and sometimes any others who may be on the periphery of the disagreement. The sulker can make things quite unpleasant in the home, in relationships or amongst groups of friends. They can often hold quite a bit of power, sometimes achieving what they set out to do and getting their own way because others around them just want to reinstate the status quo. Sulking is a passive-aggressive form of behaviour. It doesn't resolve problems and can sometimes even escalate them. Ultimately it can also be embarrassing for the sulker because they may eventually become bored with their sulking and want to stop but do not want to appear to have given in.

I can remember being in this position a few times as a child and if I eventually did give in and decide to just talk again somebody was always bound to say 'oh the sulk is over now is it?', making me feel very silly. Needless to say it is a tactic I try to avoid in adult life. There are plenty of adults out there though who are still using this conflict style to get their own way. I have encountered a number of them and I have found the best way to deal with them is the way I dealt with my children when they sulked, and that was to pretend I hadn't noticed.

Sniper

The sniper very rarely addresses the actual problem but just fires bullets from the sideline until either the person under fire submits or starts firing back. It may take the form of somebody just being snappy with you, putting you down or even openly insulting you without any obvious provocation from you or at least none that you are aware of. They are generally annoyed with you about something that they are finding difficult to put into words. Sometimes they know that their anger is unreasonable and therefore are reluctant to actually address it, so instead they cause a row over something else. The problem with being a sniper is they often don't get to address their insecurities or hurt feelings and they fester, usually breaking out in another snipe fest. The sniper very rarely recognises they are one so hopefully they will meet somebody who recognises it and can challenge them in such a way as to get them to own their feelings and talk about any perceived grievances in a productive fashion.

Pocketer

The pocketer is not entirely a style. It can be an aspect of other fight styles. It is, however, one that is fairly common. How many times have you been having an argument with somebody and said 'and another thing', throwing some past misdemeanour at them? The art of arguing productively is sticking to the point. If you are arguing about one issue it is very rarely useful to bring up past grievances. Another aspect of the pocketer is that they are often the one who says 'everyone knows you are a liar/untrustworthy/hot-headed, etc.' This is calling in the cavalry and usually means they don't feel their grievance holds enough weight to stand on its own merit. The best way to deal with the pocketer is to refuse to allow them to bring items out of their sometimes very deep pockets. Instead just remind them what you are arguing about and tell them that you are only prepared to deal with this at the moment but you are more than happy to deal with other grievances another time.

* * *

We learn our fight styles as a child, usually seeing what works with the people around us. If you grow up in a family where there are lots of arguments and the person who shouts loudest gets heard you may adopt the style of the volcano, unless you observe arguments leading to violence and then you may decide it is safer to be the ostrich. You may have discovered as a child that sulking usually got you your own way and in this case you may continue to revert to this going through life until it is challenged.

I am not a psychologist and my work with students did not involve psychological assessments. The above observations are gleaned through my work with adults, young people and personal experience.

If your teenager recognises their preferred style(s) and they examine the effect of this style on the people involved with them there is a good chance that they will have more produc-tive arguments. I really don't believe conflict is something that we should be afraid of; instead we should look at it as an opportunity for growth or change.

There are styles that will have more impact on us or upset us more than others. It is a worthwhile exercise to look at this. You can do this yourself. Ask yourself which of the above style(s) you are most likely to adopt and then ask yourself which of the styles would present the biggest problem for you. Then try to figure out why.

I came from a house where people were not afraid of an argument so raised voices do not bother me that much, that is as long as the raised voice is a female one. This is because the women in my family were all histrionic and prone to shouting but if my father raised his voice it was both quite rare and usually serious. Being a dormant volcano I recognise other volcanoes immediately and my challenge is to stifle my urge to match their behaviour - not always successfully but I am getting better. The style that would challenge me the most is the ostrich, maybe because I rightly or wrongly associate them with fence-sitters, a trait very often criticised in my family. I am also quite an impatient person, another family trait I am afraid, so I could see myself losing patience with somebody who didn't want to talk about a problem or give an opinion.

None of the above are right or wrong and you may be quite happy with the way you handle conflict, whatever your preferred style. The exercise is not necessarily to change but more to be aware of the effect of your conflict style on others and possibly make allowances for this.

DEALING WITH BREAK-UPS OR HEARTBREAK

This topic is often raised in a group and most teenagers would probably have liked me to give them the formula for pain-free break-ups. Well if I could do that I would be a very rich woman!

The fact is relationships must end and they never end well, at least not for both parties. So what do I mean by this? If a relationship ends, for whatever reason, usually one party is more hurt than the other and if a relationship does not end but develops into a lifelong, committed, happy partnership the heartbreak will come from the death of one of the partners. You might say why bother then? Well we all know that forming healthy relationships is one of if not the most important and fulfilling aspects of life. If we don't form relationships it could be due to logistics such as where we live, or it could be due to a fundamental personality issue such as crippling shyness or other more serious problems. As Shakespeare said, 'it is better to have loved and lost than never to have loved at all', although it doesn't feel like this when you are the one being left. I can certainly remember feeling that my heart was broken and believing that I had lost my one and only chance at happiness. I can also remember my sister saying 'you will get over it. It only seems important to you now; give it a few days and it will be much less important.' At the time I didn't believe her but of course it turned out to be true. Teenagers fall in and out of love very easily; that is not the same as really loving someone. That feeling of being *in love*, wanting to see them all the time, thinking about them constantly, possibly dreaming about them, not being able to keep your hands off them, etc., etc. is not love. It is infatuation, which is just another trick of

Mother Nature to get us to reproduce, but it is the hook that occasionally develops into love.

If you son or daughter is going through a break-up acknowledge their pain. The end of a relationship is not meant to be pleasant; otherwise the relationship wasn't worth having in the first place. Reassure them that the pain caused by the break-up does heal and that just because somebody wanted to end a relationship it doesn't mean that there is anything wrong with them; they are still the same person they fell in love with in the beginning. At this point, it might be useful if you have a personal example from when you were their age. If you don't have an appropriate example be inventive because stories and scenarios are far more effective than platitudes. The rule of thumb in these situations is:

- Take time to listen - you are really privileged if your teenager chooses to talk to you instead of or as well as a friend about this.
- Don't interrupt.
- Do not minimise or make light of what they are telling you. We sometimes do this as parents in the hope that this will encourage our children not to overreact, but in this case I can guarantee it will shut them down.
- Don't demonise the other party. This can just make your child feel like a victim - never useful.
- Give a personal example if you can - it doesn't have to be true.
- Ask them have they learnt anything from it and what they would like to happen next.
- Reassure them that it will get better.

Relationships, especially young, new relationships, are constantly changing and what we are looking for today is not necessarily what we will be looking for tomorrow. This time they are the ones with the broken heart; next time they may be the heartbreaker. If this is the case, encourage your teenager to treat their soon-to-be ex-partner with respect. The fact that they no longer want them for a girlfriend or boyfriend should not stop them treating them the way they would like to be treated under similar circumstances. Never end a relationship online or in a text. It is far more respectful to either talk in person face-to-face or at least have a conversation over the phone. The exception to this is if they feel the other person will not take it well and it might lead to conflict. In this case, you should suggest very strongly that they do not arrange to tell them in person.

FAMILY RELATIONSHIPS

It is no secret that teenagers can be difficult to live with. I certainly wasn't easy. Having said this, not all problems in families can be laid at their door. At the same time as our children reach teenage years we are also possibly approaching periods of transition in our own lives, such as the menopause, marriage difficulties, health problems, career problems, or our own parents becoming ill or dying. So is it any wonder that our households can become a little fraught to say the least?

So what do teenagers mean when they say they want to talk about family problems? Usually it is how to handle disagreements between them and their parents, worries about parents not getting on with each other, and pressures or perceived pressures regarding educational achievements.

Arguments and disagreement between parents and their teenage children is a much talked about topic but that does not mean we are any nearer an understanding now than when I was the teenager in question.

Teenagers are meant to push boundaries: they are becoming independent and with that they become more challenging. They are hardwired to be like this. If they weren't society would stagnate. Imagine if they never took chances or challenged widely accepted beliefs or said things that their 50-year-old self would never utter. I am sure most parents at times would welcome this but this stage in our children's development is also an opportunity for us to grow. I had the opportunity to spend a few hours with my seventeen-year-old great-nephew recently and he thought he was quite the revolutionary and was very scornful of anybody over the age of 25, except Jim Morrison, whom he admired a little too much. He really believed adults only read books like *Jane Eyre*, whereas his favourite author was Aldous Huxley, and he was quite shocked that somebody as ancient as I had also read Huxley. He reminded me of my sixteen-year-old self quoting Bob Dylan to my dad and saying things for shock value. There was a period when I was growing up when my dad did his best to stop my sister and me from listening to Bob Dylan. He thought we were going to run off to a commune or at the very least throw ourselves wholeheartedly into the 'free love generation' that was reported widely in the *News of the World* on a Sunday (much to the faux shock and salacious enjoyment of my grandmother). Well chance would have been a fine thing! I really believed at the time that my generation was the first to see through the myths peddled by older generations. The truth is though that we just see through different myths because, as Dylan said, 'The Times They Are a-Changin''. Attitudes, however, stay more or less the same. So you see it is really a rite of passage and as a parent I personally was happier for my children to challenge things rather than just blindly accepting others' beliefs.

Talk to your teenagers without trying to show them the error of their ways. Tell them about your life, your insecurities, your hopes and fears, and they may surprise you by being interested. Tell them about a time you took a risk. It makes us a lot more human to them and breaks down a little bit of the barrier that prevents good communication.

When teenagers talk about 'their parents not getting on' this can mean a myriad of things. It may be just that their parents have the odd tiff or it could be that they feel like they are constantly in a battle zone. Firstly, I don't know anybody living together with another adult who does not have at the very least 'the odd tiff'. It would be more unusual if this didn't happen than if it does. I can assure you I have had more than the odd tiff with my husband during the course of our marriage. This has fortunately been balanced with numerous periods of calm and laughter so I would suggest that you as the parent look at your relationship with your spouse/partner and objectively examine the messages that your children are picking up. You don't have to be perfect but try to be aware that you are possibly modelling unhelpful relationship behaviours. If you are going through relationship problems it might be helpful to be honest with your teenagers and tell them what you are doing to try to resolve them and give them permission to talk to you about them. Of course you don't have to divulge the intricate details of the problems; everybody is entitled to their privacy.

Normally when teenagers talk about parental pressure to do well in school and more particularly to get good exam results they do understand that a part of this pressure is their parents' desire to see them reach their full potential and they do perceive this as a positive pressure; it only becomes negative when it is unrealistic. I meet students from time to time whose parents seem to be a little deluded about their abilities. These are the students who seem to be under quite a bit of stress. When asked have they had a realistic conversation with their parents about their ability to achieve expected results some of them have and others say it would be a waste of time. If your child is struggling with a subject sometimes grinds will help but sometimes it is just wasting money. I have been there and done that. Maybe asking them about their interests, hopes and plans might make it easier for you to work together instead of the seemingly constant task of pushing water up a hill.

Finally, communication is key. Sometimes it can be easier to leave teenagers to their own resources, especially when they are resisting all attempts to involve them in family life. As stated earlier, it is normal for them to remove themselves but they generally still want to feel that they are a part of things, albeit on their own terms. So a few rules of thumb are:

- Say something positive to them at least once a day.
- Ask their opinion as often as possible.
- Apologise when you are wrong.
- Be irreverent – they love this.
- Make them laugh.
- Pick your arguments.

- Don't take yourself or them too seriously.
- Hug them at least once a day, especially when you think they least deserve it.

Final Thoughts

23

As stated at the beginning of the book, I do not purport to be an expert in child-rearing or the psychology of young people. What I have attempted to do is to give a 'fly-on-the-wall' view of my 24 years' experience of working with children and teenagers, along with some practical tips that might help. However, do feel free to ignore any tips or dismiss any opinions. I would be the very person most likely to do both of these, sometimes to my peril, but occasionally I have found a far more effective way of dealing with a problem by trying something new.

How many times have you heard that 'parenting is the hardest job in the world'? Well not without good reason. It has the longest hours, lowest pay, most responsibility and least thanks than any other job that I can think of, but it can also be the most rewarding. Don't be too hard on yourself; don't compare yourself to friends or so-called experts; and don't worry if occasionally you feel that you don't even like your offspring – as long as this is a fleeting thought due to some abominable behaviour or other it is perfectly normal. One of the truest and most amusing quotes I have read about family life is by Mary Karr, an American poet and essayist, who said, 'I think a dysfunctional family is any family with more than one person in it.'

Finally, DO NOT BE AFRAID OF MAKING MISTAKES and EXPECT YOUR CHILDREN TO MAKE MISTAKES – that is what makes us human.

Useful Contacts

Mental Health/Alcohol/Drugs
HSE Health Promotion website - useful booklets, etc.
www.healthpromotion.ie

SpunOut
www.spunout.ie
01 675 3554
hello@spunout.ie

Drugs and Alcohol Helpline
www.drugs.ie
1800 459 459
helpline@hse.ie

Crosscare Teen Counselling
www.crosscare.ie
01 8360011
info@crosscare.ie

Aware
www.aware.ie
1800 804 848
supportmail@aware.ie

Unplanned Pregnancy
My Options - free counselling (Mon-Fri, 9 a.m.-9 p.m.)
Medical advice 24 hours, 7 days
www.myoptions.ie
1800 828 010

LGBTQ+ Issues
BelongTo
www.belongto.org
01 670 6223
info@belongto.org

Gender Issues
TENI (Transgender Equality Network of Ireland)
www.teni.ie
01 873 3575
office@teni.ie

Parental Concerns
Parentline - a helpline for parents that offers a friendly ear
and non-judgemental advice from other parents
www.parentline.ie
1890 927 277/01 873 3500
info@parentline.ie

Rape/Sexual Assault
Rape Crisis Centre
www.rapecrisishelp.ie
1800 778 888

Eating Disorders
Bodywhys
www.bodywhys.ie
01 210 7906
alex@bodywhys.ie